Diversion from Custody for Mentally Disordered Offenders

Social Services Training Manuals

First Line Management: Staff by Kevin Ford and Sarah Hargreaves
Effective Use of Teambuilding by Alan Dearling
Manual on Elder Abuse by Chris Phillipson and Simon Biggs
Developing Training Skills by Tim Pickles and Howie Armstrong
Training for Mental Health by Thurstine Basset and Elaine Burrel
Monitoring and Evaluation in the Social Services by David and Suzanne Thorpe
Quest for Equality by Errol John and Barbara Deering
Care Sector Quality: A Training Manual Incorporating BS5750 by Steve Casson and Clive George

Other titles from Longman include:

On Becoming a Manager in Social Work edited by Barbara Hearn, Giles Darvill and Beth Morris
Quality Assurance for Social Care Agencies by Emlyn Cassam and Himu Gupta
NSPCC: *Child Sexual Abuse: Listening, Hearing and Validating the Experience of Children* by Corinne Wattam, John Hughes and Harry Blagg
NSPCC: *Listening to Children: The Professional Response to Hearing the Abused Child* edited by Anne Bannister, Kevin Barrett and Eileen Shearer
NSPCC: *From Hearing to Healing: Working with the Aftermath of Child Sexual Abuse* edited by Anne Bannister
NSPCC: *Making a Case in Child Protection* by Corinne Wattam
NSPCC: *Key Issues in Child Protection for Health Visitors and Nurses* edited by Christopher Cloke and Jane Naish
Making Sense of the Children Act (2nd edition) by Nick Allen
Female Sexual Abuse of Children: The Ultimate Taboo edited by Michele Elliott
Looking After Young People in the Care System by Pat Goodall, Tony Laughland, Simon Biggs and Fergus Smith
Getting Started with NVQ: Tackling the Integrated Care Awards by Barry Meteyard
Young People and Drugs: A Multi-Disciplinary Training Manual by Mike Carr and Rosie Higgins
Answers: A Handbook for Residential and Foster Carers Looking After Young People Aged 11–13 Years by Ann Wheal and Ann Buchanan

Diversion from Custody for Mentally Disordered Offenders

a practical guide

by

Catherine Staite, Neill Martin
Michael Bingham and Rannoch Daly

Routledge
Taylor & Francis Group
LONDON AND NEW YORK

First published 1994 by Longman Group Limited

Published 2017 by Routledge
2 Park Square, Milton Park, Abingdon, Oxon OX14 4RN
711 Third Avenue, New York, NY 10017, USA

First issued in hardback 2017

Routledge is an imprint of the Taylor & Francis Group, an informa business

A catalogue record for this book is available from The British Library

ISBN 13 : 978-1-138-41557-7 (hbk)
ISBN 13 : 978-0-582-23900-5 (pbk)

Typeset by The Midlands Book Typesetting Company, Loughborough, Leics.

Contents

Contributors

Catherine Staite LLB
Director, North Humberside MIND

Catherine Staite is the Director of North Humberside MIND. A lawyer by training, Catherine spent five years teaching before joining North Humberside MIND in 1990.

Catherine's particular area of interest is mental health and offending. She chairs the North Humberside Forum on Mentally Disordered Offenders and is one of the managers of the Diversion from Custody Project, based at North Humberside MIND. She is a member of the Board of Visitors at Hull Prison.

Neill Martin BA, MBA
Senior Probation Officer

Neill Martin is a Senior Probation Officer (field team). Prior to his latest appointment he was the Senior Probation Officer at HM Prison Hull for three years. Qualified since 1981, Neill has a wide experience of working with people with mental health problems who commit offences.

While working in the prison Neill contributed to the successful development of the North Humberside Diversion from Custody Project.

Michael Bingham MSc
Inspector, Humberside Police

Michael Bingham is an Inspector with Humberside Police. He has 22 years of service in a variety of areas and is currently responsible for data protection. His interest in mentally disordered offenders contributed to the development of the multi-agency forum in North Humberside and the Diversion Project.

Rannoch Daly BA
Governor, HM Prison Hull

Rannoch Daly has been the Governor of HM Prison Hull for three years. Prior to that appointment he was involved in the planning and implementation of 'Fresh Start'. He is currently developing a strategy for Hull Prison's changing role to Community Prison, which involves partnership working with other agencies. His involvement has been instrumental in the successful development of the Diversion from Custody Project.

Foreword

Tolerance and compassion which is often said, rightly or wrongly, to be a feature of our society, does not extend to people categorised as mentally disordered. Society is still uncomfortable and often fearful of people who are categorised in this way. Traditionally help from the statutory services has been poor, with a low spending priority being accorded for help to such a vulnerable group of people. If tolerance and compassion have been lacking generally for people categorised as mentally disordered, how much more so does this apply to the mentally disordered offender. Such a person appears to fulfil the expectations of society that they are less worthy than the 'average' citizen and images in the media fuel that approach and add the dimension of fear.

However, amongst people involved in the criminal justice system working with mentally disordered offenders, a change of culture is occurring. There cannot be many working in the system who do not believe that it is right to divert mentally disordered offenders from custody. This has been given added emphasis in the last few years, by the Home Office Circular in 1990 which encouraged such a policy of diversion. That was added to by the Code of Practice on the Mental Health Act 1983, first published in 1991, which refers to the vulnerability of people when in police or prison custody and drawing attention to the risk of suicide and other self harm for those detained in custody. Indeed, in the period leading up to the issue of the Home Office Circular, the number of those who committed suicide whilst held in custody and who had a history of mental health problems, including previous psychiatric in-patient admission, demonstrated very clearly why it was urgent to address the needs of this vulnerable group of people.

Those involved in this work though must understand and accept that there is a need for public safety and reassurance of the public. For Diversion Schemes ultimately to become accepted, the public has to be confident that they are not at risk by the promotion of such schemes. Equally however, the nature of the schemes, in order to achieve that confidence, must not be so tilted in favour of what society may demand, as to deprive offenders of their own rights. It is a very difficult balance. There must be certain principles on which such diversion schemes are based. At the very least these must be fairness and justice. There must also be accountability of the service. To tailor a service to meet individual needs without discrimination, to use the least restraint and confinement necessary, to provide adequate treatment and care for those who can benefit from it, and to do all this in the local community, requires flexibility and levels of co-operation between various Agencies, which traditionally have been lacking. Yet Government policy set out in the 1990 Home Office Circular has been quite explicit — namely that mentally disordered offenders should receive care and treatment from Social Services and Health Authorities in preference to the criminal justice system. Some four years later a number of different models of schemes for diversion from custody exist. There is the temptation constantly 'to re-invent the wheel' and without necessarily a clear and shared vision of how such schemes should work.

As with all schemes, the commitment must be endorsed by those operating them and not just by those planning the schemes. There are indications from all over the country that a lead in this is being given by those with the power to do so, but real change will only come about when there is a common shared vision, not only of why there is the necessity to establish such schemes, but also to answer the question — diversion from custody into what? Catherine Staite's book provides a way forward. It is now up to local agencies to provide or obtain funding to assist this vulnerable group of people.

Timothy F. Durkin
Chairman, MIND (National Association for Mental Health)

Acknowledgements

Thanks to

Andrew Cooper	—	Department of Health
Helen McKinnen	—	Home Office C.3. Division
Rhys Davies	—	National MIND
Gerald Midgely	—	Centre for Systems Studies — University of Hull

1 Why are people with mental health problems sent to prison?

Introduction

The problem of people with mental illnesses and learning disabilities in prison is not new. As early as 1835, a surgeon at Newgate Gaol was writing about it in terms so despairing as to indicate that it was not a new problem then (Grounds, 1990).

Much has been written and said on the subject. This book makes reference to some of the writing and research in this area. However, this is not a theoretical book, it is a practical guide for those working in the criminal justice system, health, social services, probation and voluntary organisations, who wish to work together to develop a system to divert people with mental health problems and learning disabilities from inappropriate remands and sentences in custody.

Aim of the book

The aim of the book is to give to practitioners and managers in all the relevant agencies, all the practical information necessary to develop a comprehensive system of multi-agency co-operative working to facilitate diversion at all points in the criminal justice system. The purpose of any diversion system should be to prevent inappropriate custodial remands and sentences. Such a system should also enable a full range of appropriate treatment, care and support to be provided.

Method

In addition to providing an overview of the way in which each agency relates to others with regard to the management of mentally disordered offenders within the system, the book also outlines models of multi-agency collaboration and suggests possible sources of funding for the development of projects.

Solutions

It is impossible to prescribe any solution which will meet the needs of mentally disordered offenders throughout the country, nor is such a solution desirable. Therefore this book gives guidance on how best to adapt models of good practice and systems used elsewhere with success to meet the particular needs of each geographical area. It also gives guidance on some of the pitfalls and potential problems which inevitably occur in any development work, and especially in development work undertaken by partnerships involving so many agencies.

Analysis of the problem

What is mental disorder?

Definition — The words 'mentally disordered offender' mean different things to different practitioners. The definition of 'mental disorder' used in this book is the same definition contained in S1(2) of the Mental Health Act (MHA) 1983:

> In this Act . . .
> 'mental disorder' means mental illness, arrested or incomplete development of mind, psychopathic disorder and any other disorder or disability of mind and 'mentally disordered' shall be construed accordingly
>
> 'severe mental impairment' means a state of arrested or incomplete development of mind which included severe impairment of intelligence and social functioning and is associated with abnormally aggressive or seriously irresponsible conduct on the part of the person concerned and 'severely mentally impaired' shall be construed accordingly
>
> 'mental impairment' means a state of arrested or incomplete development of mind (not amounting to severe mental impairment) which includes significant impairment of intelligence and

> social functioning and is associated with abnormally aggressive or seriously irresponsible conduct on the part of the person concerned and 'mentally impaired' shall be construed accordingly
>
> 'psychopathic disorder' means a persistent disorder or disability of mind (whether or not including significant impairment of intelligence) which results in abnormally aggressive or seriously irresponsible conduct on the part of the person concerned.

Men and women who have mental health problems, and/or learning disabilities and who commit offences of varying seriousness cannot be described or dealt with as if they were part of an easily recognised homogenous group. There are vast differences in behaviour and need between individuals in the broad category 'mentally disordered offender' as demonstrated by the mental health and offending matrices for unconvicted and convicted offenders, shown in Figures 1.1 and 1.2.

Link between mental disorder and offending

The link between mental disorder and offending is not always clear. The question may be asked: 'does this person offend because he or she is mentally ill, or because he or she is a bad person who happens to have a mental illness?' When an offender does not appear to present any symptoms of mental distress during the criminal justice process the issue of mental disorder may not arise. The condition may only be diagnosed on remand or after sentence. Should it be assumed that the person was mentally ill at the time of the offence and that he or she is therefore less culpable, or should he or she be treated for the mental disorder during the sentence in the same way that he or she would have been if a hitherto undiagnosed back problem developed during a prison sentence?

Treatment or imprisonment?

This is a complex issue, but it is usually better for someone with a mental health problem or learning disability to receive treatment in, or from, a specialist hospital. First, prison medical officers are usually GPs and they do not have the required training, staffing and facilities to provide appropriate care. Secondly the provisions of the MHA 1983 only apply to hospitals, so the full range of treatments and safeguards are only available in a mental hospital.

UNCONVICTED

	Serious charge	Not serious charge
Mentally disordered	Remand in custody/local secure hospital	No further action/caution/ discontinuance Community mental health services Local hospital
Not mentally disordered	RIC	Bail etc.

Figure 1.1 Mental health/offence matrix (unconvicted)

CONVICTED

	Serious charge	Not serious offence
Mentally disordered	Secure hospital RSU Local secure hospital	Community mental health Local hospital
Not mentally disordered	Prison	Community punishment

Figure 1.2 Mental health/offence matrix (convicted)

Criminal responsibility

Learning disability may not present the same difficulties in deciding when the problem began, as does mental illness. However, learning disabilities may give rise to other questions, such as 'do the usual rules of criminal responsibility apply or is this person of such low intelligence as to be incapable of understanding the nature or consequences of his or her actions?' Nevertheless, there may still be a need to protect the public from future similar actions, even though punishment, as such, is not appropriate.

If a person with a mental illness is so disabled by his/her illness that they are unable to understand what is going on around them, then the provisions of the Insanity and Unfitness to Plead Act 1991, may allow a trial of the facts after the Court have ordered a range of disposals (see Home Office (HO) Circular 93/91).

Problems — post diagnosis

It should also be borne in mind that a diagnosis of treatable mental disorder which must be made in order to obtain the appropriate treatment, may have far-reaching detrimental consequences for the offender. For example, a person may wish that his mental illness had not been raised as an issue if it results in him spending six or seven years in Rampton for an offence for which he would otherwise have only served a few months in prison. It could be argued that this could not happen now because only those presenting a grave and immediate risk are likely to be admitted to a specialist hospital. However, a diagnoses of mental illness may cause all sorts of problems in the future, for example with custody of children, housing, employment, insurance and so on.

Lack of objective test

The picture is further complicated by the absence of any objective test for mental illness. Many people who have been in the psychiatric system for a long time will have had several diagnoses during that time. The change in diagnosis may have been linked to a change in behaviour. It is more usually linked to a change of psychiatrist or a change in medical fashion. Such a change, may, however, lead to denial of treatment if the new diagnosis is one of psychopathy.

Psychopathy and treatability

Section 1 of the MHA 1983 refers to psychopathic disorders. However, a person with a psychopathic disorder may only receive treatment under the MHA 1983 if he or she is 'treatable'. Just as there is no objective test for mental illness, there is no objective test for 'treatability'.

People who present with psychopathic or behavioural disorders which are linked with offending are not popular patients. Assumptions will be made about the length of treatment time it is likely to take to make any difference to their conditions. Current mental health provision is geared to a fairly quick discharge of patients, in months rather than years. As well as resulting in 'revolving door' admissions this tends to act as a disincentive to block a bed with a patient who may take years to show any sign of improved behaviour. In the meantime, such a person may be violent, aggressive or unpleasant towards staff and other patients, leading to tensions on the ward and an unstable patient mix.

It is hardly surprising, therefore, that once a person has been labelled as an untreatable psychopath, perhaps on the basis of fairly flimsy evidence, or a brief assessment, further help from the psychiatric services will be denied, especially if the person is already in the prison system. At the same time the word 'psychopath' appearing in a report to the Court will convey the meaning 'dangerous' to the magistrate or judge. Therefore such a label not only results in the denial of psychiatric treatment, it also increases the likelihood of a custodial, as opposed to a non-custodial sentence and may also lead to a longer sentence.

Conclusion

It is difficult to get an accurate picture of the exact size and nature of the problem of mentally disordered offenders in the criminal justice system. The study of Professor J. Gunn in 1991 indicated that at that time there were 1,100 convicted prisoners nationally, suffering from mental illnesses so severe, they would warrant immediate transfer from prison to mental hospital.

A visit to the health care centre, or as they were known until recently, hospital wing, of most prisons will provide sufficient evidence that there is a serious and extensive problem of people with mental illness and mental handicap being inappropriately remanded or sentenced to custody. Successful diversion requires that services are available immediately to meet the needs of each individual, wherever they are in the criminal justice system. Such services should provide an appropriate level and mix of care, support, treatment, security and rehabilitation to meet the needs of each individual at that time as advocated by Ian Bynoe in his report *Treatment Care and Security* (1992).

The diverse and discrete nature of the criminal justice system agencies

Complexity of criminal justice system

Multi-agency working within the criminal justice system to address the problems of mentally disordered offenders presents several major problems, in addition to the questions of definition and diagnoses outlined above.

Before solutions can be developed it is necessary for all those wishing to work together to have a broad understanding of the nature and complexity of the whole of the criminal justice system (see Figure 1.3).

A system or not a system?

It has been argued that the criminal justice system is not a system at all but a series of discrete agencies which operate independently, in overlapping spheres. This seems even more true if health, social services and voluntary agencies are included in the picture.

Each agency operates within the framework of different legislation, philosophies and time-scales. Each performs a very different function, within the criminal justice system, and may also perform functions outside it. It can be argued that police forces and courts are autonomous. However, they do have to respond to outside pressure of various kinds. Each agency is responsible in a different degree to a different higher authority which tends to accentuate rather than over-come differences between agencies.

Occasionally an effort is made to provide coherent leadership on the issue of mentally disordered offenders, such as in the joint Home Office Department of Health Circular 66/90.

Agencies such as probation and social services must balance the needs of mentally disordered offenders against those of other client groups, which may seem more worthy, for example, children, young people and the elderly. For some agencies such as the police, Crown Prosecution Service (CPS) and the courts, mentally disordered offenders are not their prime responsibility, rather a peripheral irritant.

Some agencies, such as district health authorities are now charged with lead responsibility for meeting the needs of this client

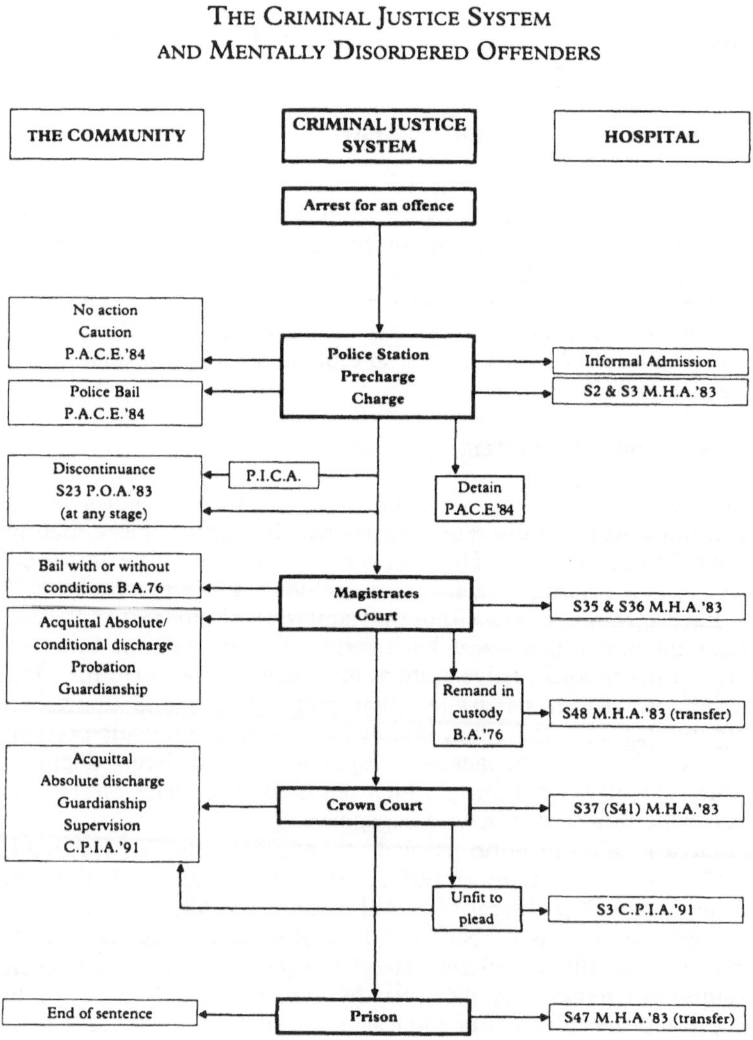

Figure 1.3 Map of criminal justice system

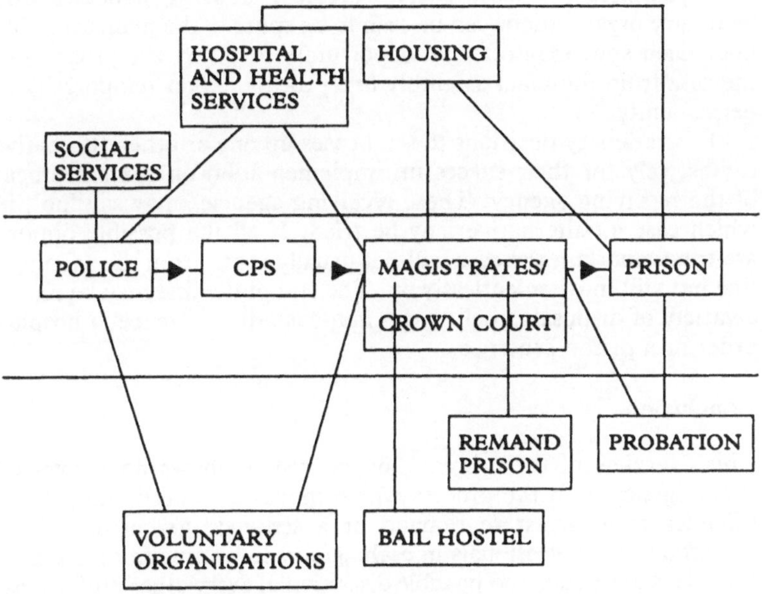

Figure 1.4 The criminal justice assembly line

group. However, health authority staff may not have a sufficient knowledge of the intricacies of the criminal justice system to know where to begin in exercising this supposed leadership.

Progress through the criminal justice system

The criminal justice system operates as a linear sort of system. One analogy is the assembly line (see Figure 1.4). Each agency along the assembly line, starting with the police and ending with the prison, deals with a particular stage of the process and dispatches the case or in some cases the actual person involved, to the next stage of the process.

The dispatching agency may have some discretion about whether to proceed and how to proceed. The police may decide to take no further action, or the CPS may decide to discontinue proceedings. In making this sort of decision each agency operates within its own discretion and without reference to the receiving agency. The receiving agency, such as the courts or the probation service has little or no control over its own work-load and must live with the consequences of decisions made by others. The prison is the ultimate example of a receiving agency.

Psychiatric services, social services, housing agencies and voluntary organisations can be seen to be spurs to the main assembly line. Each spur may offer an opportunity to divert the progress of the case from the main assembly line process, either temporarily or permanently.

Discretionary decisions to send cases up one or other alternative routes, rely for their successful implementation on the agreement of the receiving agency. These receiving agencies may say 'no', in which case an alternative may be tried. If all the possible options are tried, and fail, the case will not usually move from the assembly line but will move relentlessly on. The end of the line may be one of a variety of disposals, including a non-custodial sentence, a hospital order or a prison sentence.

Conclusion

This overview of the criminal justice system shows how involved every agency is in the process which moves a mentally disordered offender from arrest to remand or a sentence to custody. It is important for professionals in each agency to be able to understand the role, significance and possible discretion of every other professional in every other agency, not just those in close proximity to their own daily work.

Change

Each agency in the criminal justice system appears to be involved in a constant cycle of change. The purchaser/provider split in health provision has caused several years of upheaval and uncertainty and has resulted in major changes in the way in which mental health services are planned and provided. The CPS, nationally, has been re-organised. The police are facing the possibility of major changes to the way in which they are employed and rewarded. Social services departments are still getting to grips with the new care management systems imposed on them by the National Health Service and the Community Care (NHS and CC) Act 1990.

New legislation, such as the Criminal Justice Act (CJA) 1991, requires involved agencies to re-train staff, to change long-standing practice and to re-arrange priorities. When new legislation is followed swiftly by further change, as in the case of the CJA 1991, confusion reigns.

In the prevailing atmosphere of change and uncertainty, individuals within organisations tend to feel both personally and professionally insecure. Re-organisation may mean they have to re-apply for their own jobs, or that they have to adapt quickly to change, over which they have no influence or control. They may also disapprove of the change and expend a considerable amount of energy in resisting it, for a variety of personal and professional reasons.

At such times agencies tend to look inward to concentrate on the matters most pressing within their own agency, rather than outward to take a global view of problems which affect others as well as themselves. This pattern of change and the atmosphere of uncertainty which it produces, militates very strongly against the effective combination of agencies to deal with problems and issues which affect them all.

It is clear from an examination of the issues surrounding mental disorder and the criminal justice system, which must deal with the complex problems presented by mentally disordered offenders, why this has been such a constantly present problem for so many years.

Clearly, the problems are very complex and no one agency holds the key to a solution. If anything is to be achieved, all the agencies in the criminal justice system must overcome their tendency to respond to change by looking inward and learn to work together.

Need for a shared vision

In order to begin to develop a solution to the problem of mentally disordered offenders within the criminal justice system, practitioners who hope to work together must share a vision of how a diversion system should work.

Development of diversion from custody projects has tended to be piecemeal, (see Chapter 2). Projects have not always been created by partnerships of all the agencies in the criminal justice, health and social care systems, but rather by groups of a few agencies or practitioners working together without the support of all the other agencies.

This book will argue that successful diversion from custody for mentally disordered offenders can only be achieved if all relevant agencies are involved in the process. Practitioners should aim to develop not a diversion project but a diversion system.

To achieve such a system it is necessary for each involved agency to have a good understanding of the nature of other agencies' work. It is helpful to have a broad understanding of the legislative framework within which each agency operates. For example it would be useful for the practitioners from all agencies to have a working knowledge of the main sections of the Mental Health Act in order to understand the extent of, and the limitations on, the powers of mental health service providers in relation to compulsory admission. The duties of social service departments to provide community care services as laid down in the NHS and CC Act 1990 should also be understood by all other agencies.

Understanding the limitations on the freedom to act and the situations in which action is imperative by each agency is a pre-requisite of successful multi-agency working.

If each agency has unreasonable or unrealistic expectations of what others can deliver it will be impossible to design a successful system to divert mentally disordered offenders from custody.

It is impossible that all practitioners in all agencies will share identical views on the most desirable outcome for every mentally disordered offender. Differences in perspective and opinion exist between practitioners in the same agency, who have had the same professional training, and who are united by a common ethos. It is, therefore, to be expected that even greater differences in expectations about desirable outcomes will exist between for example, a CPS solicitor and a Community Psychiatric Nurse (CPN). Nevertheless each agency which participates in the development of a diversion system must agree, at a very basic level, what it is they hope to achieve.

This book suggests that the simple aims of any diversion system should be to: divert mentally disordered offenders from (1) prosecution, (2) remand in custody, (3) sentence to custody, and (4) to prevent re-offending. The shared vision of all the agencies of a diversion system which would achieve these aims should underpin all stages of the development of the system. Each individual practitioner will have his or her own view of how a system should operate in relation to the work of his or her own agency. Before these separate functions can be connected to form a diversion system, a process must first be gone through which identifies what such a connection should achieve.

2 Development of diversion projects nationally

Recent years have seen the development of a variety of types of project and scheme, reflecting different approaches to solving the problem of mentally disordered offenders in the criminal justice system.

In October 1990 the Home Office issued a circular, 66/90 which provided a lead for local agencies on dealing with the problem of mentally disordered offenders within the criminal justice system. The circular highlighted four examples of diversion schemes then in operation including the North West Hertfordshire Assessment Panel Scheme, and the Psychiatric Assessment Service at Bow Street and Great Marlborough Street Magistrates Courts. Many recent developments in diversion have drawn on the experience highlighted in those examples.

In November 1990, a joint review of health and social services provided in England for mentally disordered offenders was established under the chairmanship of Dr John Reed, Senior Principal Medical Officer, Department of Health (the Reed Committee). The final summary report (cm 2088) was published in November 1992. Eleven advisory reports have also been published, covering a wide range of issues including race, gender and equal opportunities and learning disabilities.

Continued ministerial support has been expressed for the principle recommendation that wherever possible mentally disordered offenders should be cared for and treated by health and social services rather than in the criminal justice system, and

(i) With regard to the quality of care and proper attention to the needs of the individuals:

(ii) As far as possible in the community rather than institutional settings.

(iii) Under conditions of no greater security than is justified by the degree of danger they present to themselves or to others.
(iv) In such a way as to maximise rehabilitation and their chances of sustaining an independent life.
(v) As near as possible to their own homes and families if they have them.

In Part Two of the report entitled *The Entry of Mentally Disordered People into the Criminal Justice System and the Opportunities for Diversion and Discontinuance*, the Community Advisory Group concluded:

> We have been encouraged by the initiatives taken in various parts of the country to improve prospects for diverting mentally disordered offenders from the criminal justice system to health and social services provision. The Home Office Circular 66/90 has provided a valuable stimulus to the whole process, but much more needs to be done through central and local action and inter-agency collaboration to ensure nationwide availability of effective mechanisms for assessment and diversion. Further progress is crucially important if many mentally disordered offenders are not to be drawn too far into the criminal justice system or deprived of the opportunity to receive the care, treatment and support that they may need in hospital or in the community.

The report continues:

> there should be nationwide provision of court psychiatric or similar schemes for assessment and diversion of mentally disordered offenders. These should be based on a clear local understanding as to the contribution of each agency and where the lead responsibility lies.
>
> Of great encouragement for the future are the various initiatives outlined at Annexes B and C to Circular 66/90, for providing court-based duty psychiatrist schemes or inter-agency assessment panels.
>
> **Paragraph 2.29:**
>
> There are 105 Magistrates Courts Committees in England mostly overseeing more than one Court. We envisage that assessment and diversion schemes will usually be developed at committee level. We understand that some 69 panel schemes are currently in various stages of development and that 24 of these are operational.

Recent Home Office research by Carol Hedderman indicates that there are in fact only eight panel schemes in operation. A number of other informal and partial network arrangements are also in existence. The discrepancy in number could be accounted for by these arrangements being referred to loosely as panel schemes, when they are actually court diversion schemes Alternatively, it may be that early attempts to establish schemes which were reported to the Committee, did not come to fruition or foundered through lack of funding or support.

A survey conducted by Michael Bingham (1992) of the 43 police forces in England and Wales in 1992 revealed quite different statistics to those quoted at Paragraph 2.29. Information provided identified only as operational schemes 12 force areas, with further schemes planned at that particular time in only another 13 force areas.

The reason for the discrepancy between the figures provided by police areas, may be as a result of a lack of collaboration and information exchange between agencies. Other schemes initiated by different agencies but not operating in liaison with the police service may have been in existence. This may indicate the very restricted nature of inter-agency collaboration, which does not include the police, in some areas, or poor communication within some police forces.

Following the publication of Circular 66/90 there has certainly been a substantial increase in the number of diversion schemes established. These developments have tended to be local and piecemeal rather than based on a coherent national strategy.

Innovation in health and social services is often driven by the work of individuals who help to create an environment for change and then to work hard to make the changes work. This contribution by individuals with vision is vital to the process of change and improvement in services. However, change which relies for its successful implementation too heavily on the commitment of individuals is always going to be vulnerable.

Unless such development is supported by the management within individual agencies, it will be vulnerable to the conflicting demands of routine work and to total loss if the committed individual changes post. The short-term or uncertain nature of the funding for diversion schemes has also contributed to the vulnerability of such schemes.

Although not perhaps meant as models for development in other parts of the country, the four schemes highlighted in Circular 66/90 have been widely copied. Although there is much to be said for not reinventing the wheel and basing new developments on the sound footing of others' experience, there are also numerous pitfalls and drawbacks.

First, the needs of different populations vary so widely. What is likely to be useful and effective in a large city will be wholly inappropriate in a sparsely populated rural area. Secondly, before any useful developments can be made towards establishing an effective diversion system, a substantial amount of work needs to be done by all the agencies and practitioners who will have to make the diversion scheme work. By attempting to graft a diversion scheme which is the product of much preparation and negotiation in one area onto an unprepared and uncommitted group in another area, those involved are setting themselves up to fail.

The complexity of the issues around diversion from custody and the varied levels, for example of knowledge between agencies about the relevant legal framework and the availability of alternative services to custody, combine to create an atmosphere of nervousness and uncertainty among those charged by 66/90 with beginning the work of developing diversion projects.

It is not surprising, therefore, that the temptation to copy what has been done by others with some success may become overwhelming. However, such a temptation should be resisted and instead the emphasis should be placed on designing a system which really meets the needs of each area.

It may be useful to review the progress of other schemes and the problems they have encountered in order to incorporate successful good practice into the scheme and to avoid mistakes which have proved costly in other areas.

Panel schemes

Without doubt the forerunner to all of the schemes currently in existence is the North West Hertfordshire Scheme which was established in 1985 as an experimental project and pioneered by Dorothy Tonak, a Probation Officer with the Hertfordshire Probation Service.

It was recognised at that time that an unco-ordinated approach of different agencies resulted in several difficulties, including; ambiguous reports being placed before the courts because of an inadequate process of assessment before the preparation of probation and psychiatric or psychological reports for the courts, or because of differing diagnosis, e.g. from prison and local psychiatrist. There was often conflict between psychiatric hospital admission and the inability of the community-based services to cope with disturbed or offending behaviour. It was also recognised that offenders inappropriately received prison sentences because community resources were not available or not planned by the agencies involved.

The aims of the Hertfordshire scheme were:

1. To provide a better service to the courts.
2. To improve the management of the disordered offender.
3. To mobilise resources for those individuals in the community.
4. To avoid taking on inappropriate clients for statutory supervision by the probation service.
5. To improve diagnostic skills.
6. To prevent him/her from further offending which could result in a prison sentence.
7. To prevent the disordered offender breaking down and thus being unable to function in the community which could result in a further admission to hospital.
8. To encourage the growth of a multi-disciplinary approach.

When a psychiatric report was called for by the court, a panel meeting of those likely to be involved in the future management of the case would be arranged, so that a management strategy and package of care could be arranged. The panel operated on an *ad-hoc* basis, with membership varying according to the nature of the mental disorder and the range of other problems.

The offender would be seen by the Psychiatrist or Psychologist and the Probation Officer together with the offenders own General Practitioner, Community Psychiatric Nurse (CPN) and a Social Worker.

A panel such as that described provides an opportunity for developing a multi-agency strategy, a better quality diagnosis, together with a care programme and a complete package of care and support to enable the offender to remain in the community. These arrangements could include housing with support, day care, out-patient treatment, social skills, training and so on.

Management of the case is, therefore, one of joint responsibility and gives the courts confidence to dispose of the case other than by way of a prison sentence.

Following the development of the Hertfordshire panel scheme, the Home Office funded the secondment of Dorothy Tonak, Probation Officer and Colin Bloodworth, a Community Psychiatric Nurse, to an independent trust, the Hertfordshire Care Trust to enable the two founder members of the Hertfordshire scheme to travel all over the country promoting the panel assessment scheme model, through presentations at seminars and conferences. This work helped local areas to focus on the issue of developing new approaches to the problems of mentally disordered offenders.

Although this promotional work informed a large number of practitioners it has resulted in a surprisingly small number of schemes. This may be because no new funding was identified to enable panel schemes to be established. Those which have been developed recently such as the schemes in Reading and Bolton relied at their outset on the commitment of key individuals who undertook the work of co-ordinating and operating panels in addition to their existing duties.

Not only is it inappropriate to overburden individuals with work this way, it also gives a precarious and uncertain basis for development. Thus when the committed individual changes job, the person who comes into their new post does not assume their extra responsibilities. Although the Hertfordshire scheme was first started in 1985, it has not operated continuously since then. Because it was developed with little management support, it was founded on co-operation between key individuals rather than an inter-agency collaboration.

The lack of proper funding to enable full time co-ordinators to be employed is likely to prove fatal to many panel schemes. This is extremely wasteful. Not only does the area which was served by a panel scheme loose when a scheme ceases to exist, but all the hard work, energy and commitment which will have been expended by key individuals will also be wasted.

Benefits of panel schemes

Improved communications

One of the most important elements of the panel assessment approach is communication. Agencies and practitioners who had previously often dealt with their own work and made their decisions in isolation, or at least without discussing the problems and issues fully with a wide range of colleagues, were brought together regularly to consult with and to listen to each other.

Joint responsibility

Another element which made panel assessment such a significant development was the acceptance of joint responsibility for the mentally disordered offender among participants which was fundamental to this way of working.

Drawbacks of panel schemes

Working arrangements — not systems

Panel assessment schemes are not diversionary systems as such, they are working arrangements which facilitate communications between agencies and practitioners. It is interesting that the aims of the original scheme tried to meet so many various needs. The needs of the mentally disordered offender to be diverted from custody was not paramount. Instead the aims of the scheme focused on the needs of professionals. While there is no doubt that a system of communication and co-operation which enables mental health and criminal justice practitioners to work more efficiently, make better decisions and more effective use of their time, will indirectly benefit mentally disordered offenders, the main aims of any diversion system should be to divert mentally disordered offenders from custody.

Piecemeal service

Panel schemes are currently operating in eight out of fifty-five probation service areas nationally. In only two schemes is the service available to the whole probation area. In six schemes a Probation Officer co-ordinates the panels, in the other two a member of staff from the local social services department undertakes the role of co-ordinator.

In only one of the areas is the co-ordinator full time. In three areas the co-ordinator was part-time and in the other three areas the work of co-ordinating the panels was done by practitioners to whom no time was allocated and who still had to fulfil all the routine duties of their full-time posts.

Co-ordinating meetings of a fluctuating group of practitioners from several agencies is a time consuming task for the co-ordinator. Someone must take responsibility for photocopying and distributing relevant material, verifying information, minuting meetings, writing letters, chasing up reports and so on.

Relating only to part of the criminal justice system

In addition to the problems engendered by insufficient resources being available to co-ordinate and service the panels effectively, the panel schemes are also limited in their operation in relation to the whole of the criminal justice system. Six out of the eight schemes operating provide information to the police, CPS, Magistrates and Crown Courts. Of the other two, one had no referrals from the police and the other did not involve the CPS. Only two areas had Psychiatrists attending at Court to do assessments. In order to operate effectively as a system for diversion, any scheme or arrangement must relate to the whole of the criminal justice system.

By not involving the police, the opportunities to divert from the police station, such as S2 admission under MHA 1983 are lost. By not communicating information to the CPS which could influence a decision to discontinue prosecution, a further possible opportunity for diversion is also lost. By not having a Psychiatrist available to Court on a regular basis, an opportunity to divert mentally disordered offenders to hospital under S35 MHA 1983 is lost. Expert evidence relating to risk and dangerousness will not be available to magistrates to influence decisions on remand.

Psychiatric assessment at court

Psychiatric assessment schemes operate using Psychiatrists or CPNs at Magistrates Courts all over the country, including Birmingham, Sheffield, Bradford and Hull, and at Horseferry Road, Great Marlborough Street, Bow Street and Clerkenwell among others.

Home Office Circular 66/90 and the Reed Report draw attention to the usefulness of psychiatric assessment at Court, in identifying people with mental health problems and enabling them to be diverted from the criminal justice system. The report by Dr Philip Joseph (1992) of the establishment of a psychiatric assessment scheme at Great Marlborough Street and Bow Street Magistrates Court gives a clear and readable account of how such a scheme can operate.

The Psychiatrist attended Court on two mornings a week and assessed those people who were referred by Magistrates, Clerks, Solicitors and Gaolers as possibly having some form of mental disorder. The assessments took place in the cell area, sometimes outside the cell, but sometimes through the wicket in the cell door. Rating scales were used to measure social functioning. These scales were chosen for their speed of completion because of the extremely difficult circumstances in which the assessments were carried out. The Psychiatrist was under pressure from other Court users both in the space used for assessments and the time available to undertake them.

Philip Joseph's study shows how successful psychiatric assessment can be in diverting mentally disordered offenders from unnecessary or inappropriate remands in custody. Similar schemes at Horseferry Road and Clerkenwell Magistrates Courts have also proved useful. A study of the Clerkenwell scheme showed that the average time spent on remand by mentally disordered offenders was reduced from fifty days to eight.

The success of these schemes has been in some measure due to the commitment and perseverance of the psychiatrists themselves and the co-operation of key professionals such as the Approved

Social Worker (ASW). The ability and willingness of all the professionals involved at the Court stage to respond positively and flexibly to the schemes is crucial to their success.

Dr Joseph noted in his report on the Bow Street and Great Marlborough Street schemes 'there was not a set formula for achieving inter-agency co-operation. The whole assessment enterprise relied on goodwill and a willingness to be flexible and work towards a common goal'.

The problems which can arise when co-operation is not forthcoming were exemplified by the difficulties described by Dr Joseph which arose as a result of variable co-operation of the two sets of Gaolers at the different Courts. More significant and potentially more destructive was the unhelpful response of some of the hospitals which accepted admissions from Courts. The difference in approach taken to admissions under civil and criminal sections of the MHA 1983 resulted in absurd situations. Such differences in response are influenced by the reluctance of the staff in some acute wards of accepting admissions from Court. There is often a tendency to assume that people admitted from Court require the specialist intervention of forensic psychiatry. However, the Mental Health and Offending Matrix (Figures 1.1 and 1.2) in Chapter 1 show that the issues are not clear cut.

A problem may also arise when the admission ward is full. The hospital may only be able to admit if it discharges someone less seriously ill. However, the consequence for the discharged patient, if he or she does not have adequate care and support in the community, may be a deterioration which leads to offending. Thus the problem has been moved, but not solved.

The most striking thing about psychiatric assessment in Court is the way in which one specialist professional function, the assessment of a person's mental health by a psychiatrist, is constricted and confined by the demands of the criminal justice system.

Victorian magistrates courts have cells which are almost medieval in their lack of daylight, fresh air and space. In such an environment, in a very confined space, the Court Psychiatrist will try to assess an unknown individual who may have profound difficulties with communication, or not even speak English. The interview cell is noisy and airless. There is a constant noise and disruption coming and going in the cell area. Psychiatrists must compete for space with Defence Solicitors, and for time with the demands of the Court list and the transport timetable of those responsible for the movement of prisoners. This situation demonstrates the imbalance in the authority between services devoted to the welfare of the individual, such as the health service, social services and probation, and services existing to serve the public interest, such as the police, Courts and CPS. Thus the function of psychiatric assessment is obliged to restrict itself to the space and time allowed by the demands of the criminal justice system if it is to operate within the system at all.

Psychiatric assessment in these conditions can be useful in identifying those people whose mental health problem or learning disability is sufficiently severe to warrant immediate admission under the civil sections of the MHA 1983. However, if those people could be identified at the police station they could be diverted from there and avoid the trauma of Court altogether. The most useful contribution of Court psychiatric assessment schemes to diversion is in cases where it is obvious that there is something wrong with the defendant but he or she does not fall easily into any particular diagnostic category. In difficult or complex cases admission wards may be reluctant to admit people from the Courts under civil sections because of a widely held suspicion that in cases of doubt the health service is expected to cope with people who are not actually 'treatable' under the MHA 1983, or who are so disruptive and challenging as to be unmanageable on an open ward.

However, admissions under S35 can be made in cases where there is no clear diagnoses and where a full assessment could help to identify whether someone could usefully be treated under another section. The great advantage of an S35 admission is that the time scale is so flexible. If it becomes apparent fairly quickly that the person is not treatable under the Act, the case can be referred back to the Court for an alternative disposal to be made.

In order for the Magistrates Court to make an S35 order, it is necessary to have both psychiatric evidence available to the Court that an assessment in hospital is necessary and confirmation that a bed is available. Therefore, S35 admissions require a Psychiatrist at Court who has an admission arrangement with Psychiatrists responsible for general admissions wards.

Psychiatric assessment schemes must be properly organised in order to be successful. The time spent in Court should be part of a Psychiatrist's job description, rather than the result of an informal arrangement based on good will or personal commitment. The Court Psychiatrist's role also needs to be covered for sick leave and holidays.

One way to organise a scheme is to have a rota of Psychiatrists who take it in turns to do a session at Court on a particular day each week. This has several advantages, firstly it shares the burden of what can be very stressful work in very difficult surroundings. It also ensures that responsibility for mentally disordered offenders is not confined solely to Forensic Psychiatrists. Access to ordinary psychiatric services can be gained for people who may previously have been thought too demanding or challenging for them, Psychiatrists can cover for each other during absences and can also use each other as a resource if assessing people whose particular problems are a specialisation of one of the other rota members, for example drug or alcohol abuse or learning disability. Clear arrangements need to be made to ensure that the rota works effectively.

Funding the rota can be done in a variety of ways. The Home Office may be willing to provide initial or continued funding to set up schemes where Psychiatrists or CPNs undertake assessments at Court. However, the scope of funding is limited and will not cover travel expenses, secretarial support or salaries relating to time not spent in Court. District health authorities have recently been instructed by their respective regional health authorities to take a lead in developing services which enable mentally disordered offenders to be diverted from custody. They may therefore be willing to fund that part of the costs of a Psychiatrists rota at Court not covered by Home Office funding or even to cover the whole costs.

Examination of the operation of panel schemes and Court assessment schemes reveals that however successful they are in intervening at a particular point in the criminal justice system, they are not easily able to adapt or develop to intervene at other points in the criminal justice system.

However, it may be possible to piece together a set of existing separate diversion arrangements to form a complete diversion system operating at different stages in the system. It may be easier and more productive to enhance existing arrangements than to start again with a new system.

Certainly, areas which already have some form of scheme operating can use it as a basis for further development to provide intervention at every possible point in the criminal justice system.

North Humberside diversion from custody project

Aims

The aims of the North Humberside Diversion from Custody Project are to divert mentally disordered offenders from prosecution, from remand to custody and from sentence to custody. The project also aims to help prevent re-offending. The development of the project followed the advice contained in Home Officer/Department of Health Circular 66/90.

Working methods

The project is based in the central offices of North Humberside MIND, in Hull. The project team is made up of an Approved Social Worker, a Community Psychiatric Nurse and a Probation Officer. Together they seek to achieve the aims of the project by intervening at every decision making point in the criminal justice system to enable non-custodial disposals to be made.

In January 1994 the project expanded its services to cover Courts and police stations in rural areas in North Humberside. The development was made possible by funding from the Home Office and local health purchasers, East Riding Health, for an additional CPN post.

The CPN covering rural areas, telephones each of the three police stations which hold prisoners overnight to find out who is in custody. He then checks names against those on the Diversion database using his laptop computer.

He then travels to whichever rural Court is sitting that day. When more than one is sitting he will go to the busiest and follow up those people identified as being in custody. Where there may be mentally disordered offenders at more than one court, he will refer those at the Court, other than the one he is going to, to the Court Probation Officer.

The development of the project in rural East Yorkshire and Holderness requires the support and assistance of other agencies to succeed.

The team start their day at 7.30 a.m. by visiting each of the three Hull police stations in order to identify and assess any mentally disordered offenders in custody, at the earliest point possible in the criminal justice system. The team liaise with custody officers to facilitate diversion, where possible.

At 8.45 a.m. the team meet at Hull Magistrates Court where they pool information on their separate visits to the police stations. They then assess prisoners in the Court cells, decide priorities and allocate work in the Courts. By 9.30 a.m. they are ready to consult with the Crown Prosecution and Defence Solicitors. They offer advice and information and will make arrangements for appropriate housing or bail support to avoid the necessity of a remand or sentence to custody. Each team member then follows through his individual case work during the Court day. They may be called to give evidence that a particular defendant is known to the project and that they will make such arrangements for that person as the Court considers necessary in order to grant bail. One team member has special responsibility for liaising with prison staff and taking referrals from HM Prison Hull and the Wolds Remand Prison. The team meet up at the end of the day in their own office to exchange information and to plan for the following day. They work together collectively and collaboratively pooling their individual knowledge and expertise to provide a responsive and effective service. Some functions may only be performed by one of them, for example, only the ASW may be involved in an admission to hospital under a section of the Mental Health Act, otherwise there is no distinction between their three professions within the project.

As the project developed it became apparent that some input from a psychiatrist was necessary especially to do assessments at Court. Following a successful bid to the Home Office for funding, a rota of Psychiatrists is now being organised for each Tuesday morning. Where remands in custody for a psychiatric report are unavoidable they need now be for no more than six days.

Diversion can take place from any decision point in the criminal justice process from arrest to post-sentence. Ideally diversion should take place as early as possible after arrest. Most diversions are to community based services rather than to hospital.

This pattern of diversion highlights a trend of referrals which come mainly from the criminal justice agencies resulting mainly in diversion to health and social services as recommended in Home Office Circular 66/90. This transfer of responsibility from one area of the statutory sector to another has serious resource implications (see Chapter 6, 'Diversion into what?').

When a person's mental health is giving cause for concern but where it is difficult to make an adequate diagnosis during an ordinary assessment interview on day one, a person may be remanded in custody to appear the following Tuesday to be assessed by the Rota Psychiatrist.

The team will spend that first period of remand putting together an effective package of care including residential accommodation. If the Court is satisfied with these arrangements the person may be bailed at second appearance.

The project team members support mentally disordered offenders on bail and keep in touch with those in prison and hospital. If the disposal is non-custodial, arrangements are made with community mental health teams if necessary for continued support. If custody is the outcome the team will explore the possibility of transfer from prison to hospital under S47 of the Mental Health Act 1983 and make arrangements for support on release.

Under S38 of the Police and Criminal Evidence Act 1984 it is the duty of the police when interviewing a person perceived as vulnerable about an alleged offence to ensure that s/he is accompanied by an Appropriate Adult.

In partnership with Humberside Police the project has designed a training course which is being repeated regularly. The trained Appropriate Adults are being registered in order that the police can have access to an Appropriate Adult at any time one is needed. Before leaving the police station the Appropriate Adult faxes the relevant information to the project who pick up the referral at the start of the next working day.

The Diversion project has developed a data-base on which is stored all the relevant information relating to clients of the project. The data base is updated daily. Each member of the Diversion team has a laptop computer. This enables each team member to have access to the data-base, wherever he or she is.

Each team member has a mobile phone and a bleep. This enables them to keep in touch with the office and each other.

The first year of the project was evaluated by the Hull University Centre for Systems Studies. The project had achieved a diversion rate of 85 per cent of 124 cases by the end of its first full year of operation.

Adapting the experience of other areas

Each of the models outlined has advantages and disadvantages. Practitioners working together to develop a diversion system can learn a great deal from the experience of others. However, it is important not to succumb to the temptation to copy wholesale.

There are several reasons why simply copying a model which has proved successful elsewhere is not advisable. Firstly, the project or system may not be as successful as its proponents would like. It may have serious flaws or operational problems which are never aired publicly. By copying such a project practitioners may well be perpetuating those unresolved issues. Before adopting systems and practices which appear to work elsewhere the steering group should send representatives to visit the project they are thinking of copying, and read very carefully any independent evaluation which is available.

The second major reason for not copying other projects is that systems and networks which work well in urban areas will not translate to rural areas. There are also substantial differences in need between very large cities and other types of urban area. These differences do not only relate to the size of the population, but also to all the other factors such as, for example, availability of alternatives to custody, transport, large ethnic minorities and poverty.

The most pressing reason for not copying too closely projects and systems from other parts of the country is that by doing so the steering group will miss a vital opportunity to instil a sense of ownership of the project in local agencies. There is always resistance to imported ideas, especially if ideas are imported across the North-South divide or from London to the rest of the country.

The process of designing a diversion system to meet local needs has many benefits which should more than repay the effort involved. The process will be a learning exercise for all the agencies in the criminal justice system about the work of other agencies with which they do not normally come in contact. It will enable practitioners to exchange ideas and build networks. It will also help to stimulate local debate about how best to meet unmet need.

By designing their own system rather than copying an existing system the steering group can look at different models tried in other areas, and test them to see whether they would meet local need. This process should involve every member of the steering group, who may wish to bring in other colleagues to look closely at particular areas of difficulty. At the end of the process the steering group should have a diversion system which may utilise the experience and build on the success of other schemes, but which is essentially designed to meet local need.

One of the advantages enjoyed by steering groups looking at designing a system for their area is the wealth of previous experience now available to draw on. In the late 1980s those working in Diversion were pioneers, promoting ideas which seemed very new and challenging. Practitioners looking at new diversionary systems now are operating in a climate which is much more open to the development of new and radical approaches to what was often viewed in the past as an insoluble problem.

Opportunities for development of diversion schemes

The creation of a climate for change which began with Circular 66/90 and continued with the establishment of the Reed Committee, has enabled a wide range of developments to take place. Attention continues to be focused on the needs of mentally disordered offenders.

The Health of the Nation strategy published in 1993 required health authorities to include secure and non-secure services in their strategic and purchasing plans. Services for mentally disordered offenders are a 'first order' priority for 1994/5 (EL (93)54).

> NHS authorities should work with personal social services and criminal justice agencies to develop strategic and purchasing plans for services for mentally disordered offenders and similar people, based on the joint Department of Health/Home Office review of services. These should include:

— an effective range of non-secure and secure services (including those for patients with special or differing needs such as people with learning disabilities and psychopathic disorders, ethnic minorities, young people and women.
— arrangements for the multi-agency assessment and, as necessary, diversion of offenders from the criminal justice system.
— meeting the mental health care needs of transferred or discharged prisoners.
— the placement within six months of special hospital patients who no longer require high security.

The Department of Health estimated in February 1994 that there were about one hundred court assessment and diversion schemes operating in England, of which 29 were being assisted by Home Office funding of psychiatric and nursing input, 24 schemes received financial assistance from the Department of Health in 1992/3 and 37 in 1993/4. This suggests an increasing level of activity in Court-based diversion.

Liaison between the health services and prison service has also benefited from this climate for change. Transfers of mentally disordered people from prison to hospital rose from 325 in 1990 to 755 in 1993.

One substantial area of weakness in this broadly hopeful national picture has been the inadequate response of some local authority social service departments. A recent survey by the Social Services Inspectorate of local authority community care plans showed that only half (35 of 72 examined) had included services for mentally disordered offenders. This is especially disappointing in the light of the progress made by health purchasers and providers. As we propose in Chapter 6, diversion from custody is the beginning of the solution to the problem of mentally disordered offenders, not the end. The provision of adequate day care and suitable supported accommodation is vital to the success of diversionary activity. Without it, much of the work of diversion schemes nationally will be providing temporary, not permanent solutions to the problems of mentally disordered offenders.

3 Turning the vision into reality

The first stage of this process is for practitioners to work together to design an 'ideal system'. 'Ideal', in this context does not mean unrealistic or Utopian. It means that in designing an ideal system, practitioners identify the best possible practice which their respective services can achieve and deliver.

The process of designing an ideal system enables each agency to identify those issues and problems which currently hinder diversion. Is the problem a shortage of bail hostel places? Are people being remanded in custody for long periods for psychiatric reports? Are people's problems not being recognised early enough? Can each agency make any changes locally to the way in which it operates in order to overcome these problems, or are they matters which are beyond local control? There is always a tendency when approaching an issue as complex and difficult to resolve as the problem of mentally disordered offenders in prison, to concentrate on the obstacles to successful outcomes. This concentration on difficulties can make them appear unresolvable.

Instead, when working together to design an ideal diversion system, practitioners should recognise problems but then move on to concentrate on identifying solutions.

Designing and developing a system

This task can be started by a group of concerned practitioners joining forces and organising a one-day conference involving all agencies locally. Participants need to be sufficiently senior to be able to make the initial commitment to work together. Participants need to identify what they expect from each other in multi-agency working on diversion from custody. This can be done in a variety of abstract or concrete ways.

The conference

It is useful to have one or more outside speakers who can give an overview of the current situation regarding mentally disordered offenders. The delegates can then divide into groups to analyse the problems which exist locally, perhaps by using a case study exercise which contains several of the most typical problems encountered by practitioners attempting to divert mentally disordered offenders from custody (see Appendix I). Participants can then move on to highlighting where the gaps in services and communication exist and finally to developing an idealised design of a system of diversion which would meet all the needs identified in the earlier sessions.

Development of the steering group

Mandate/authority from the conference

At the end of the conference, the membership of a steering group to develop the system should be agreed. Any group which hopes to carry forward the work of such a conference should have an informal mandate from the agencies and practitioners involved in the conference. Before long the steering group may have to approach those agencies for funding, or those practitioners to develop new working practices. Therefore, the informed consent of the participants at the conference to the composition and remit of the steering group are essential to the success of its future work. It is much easier to obtain this consent and agree on a workable remit at the end of a day spent focusing on the complexity of the problems and the pressing need for solutions, then by approaching individuals separately.

Overcoming reluctance/opposition

There is always a risk inherent in asking such a diverse group for its whole-hearted support. Several people attending the conference could be determined to oppose any change, because of professional insecurity or even personal rivalry. Change is not always welcome. The call for change may imply that those who operate the existing system, which so obviously fails to divert mentally disordered offenders from custody, have themselves failed in some way. This implication or any attempt to apportion blame, may result in defensiveness and lack of co-operation among some participants at the conference, which may be an obstacle to the steering group beginning the task of developing a system of diversion with the necessary support.

The easiest way to overcome this difficulty is to avoid it happening in the first place. It may be tempting to lay the blame for the current inadequacies of local diversion arrangements at the door of one or two individual practitioners or agencies. Even if this reflects the true situation, and the situation is rarely so simple, it is not helpful. It merely exacerbates the tendency of each agency to blame others or to regard principal responsibility as lying elsewhere.

If a lack of support from certain practitioners or agencies does seem to be a problem, then they must be appealed to on the very valid grounds that no system can be developed successfully or operated satisfactorily without their support and co-operation. Another approach is to ask the reluctant individual or agency to take a key role. Most people and organisations find it difficult to resist the twin lures to involvement of emphasis on their significance to the success of change, and the opportunity to have a key role in designing the change.

Such persuasions need to be applied with caution. First, it has to be recognised the truly Luddite individual can sometimes be impervious to all blandishments and inducements to embrace change willingly, in which case they had better not be involved at all. Secondly, although it may be tempting to ensure the co-operation of an unco-operative individual or agency by offering the position of Chair of the steering group to that individual or lead agency status to the agency, such expediency may cause more problems then it solves.

Choosing the right Chair

Whoever is chosen to chair the steering group must have sufficient professional seniority and personal standing to ensure the support of all the agencies. He or she must also be prepared to work hard. Co-ordinating and servicing a multi-agency steering group involving representatives from agencies as diverse as the police and the health authority, requires vision, tact, firmness, determination, the ability to listen, and an ability to unite others. The Clerk to the Justices has been suggested as an ideal person to perform this function. However, the profession of the person chosen to chair is less significant than the ability to enable others to work together effectively.

Membership of the steering group

The membership of the steering group should be decided at the end of the conference, if possible. The level of seniority appropriate should also be decided at this stage.

It will be difficult to maintain the interest of a Police Chief Superintendent in a steering group if the local mental health service provider trust is represented by a CPN, or the Probation Service by a main grade Probation Officer.

Because the work of the steering group will be focused on agency policy and practice, it is appropriate for each agency to nominate someone of sufficient seniority to have an overview of the service provided by his/her own agency, and a good understanding of the whole of the criminal justice system.

Steering group members also need the explicit support of their chief officers. It will be impossible to introduce changes in working practice or procedures without the commitment of chief officers to the establishment of a diversion system in their area.

However, although steering group members should be senior enough to operate effectively at a strategic multi-agency level, they should not be so lofty as to be out of touch with the realities and difficulties of the everyday working life of practitioners within their own agencies.

Development of a diversion system

Position Papers

When designing a new system to divert mentally disordered offenders from custody it is easy to be disheartened by the size and complexity of the problem. However, a good way to start is to review whatever is already available. If each agency contributes information on how it currently deals with mentally disordered offenders, it will be easier to identify where there are gaps in service provision, where there is inadequate communication between key agencies, and where extra training is needed.

Basic information about how services are already operating can be obtained by asking each agency representative on the steering group to produce a Position Paper setting out how cases involving mentally disordered offenders are dealt with. The Position Papers should contain details of the processes involved and of the significant legislation, or guidance which dictates or informs the way in which a particular agency responds to the needs of mentally disordered offenders.

In addition to their powers under the MHA 1983, the police Position Paper should refer to the Police and Criminal Evidence Act (PACE) 1984, as well as Code C of the PACE Code of Practice. The CPS Position Paper should refer to the CPS Code for Crown Prosecutors which gives clear guidance on the circumstances in which it is appropriate to discontinue proceedings. Social services departments should refer to their duties under the NHS and CC Act 1990 to assess the needs of people with mental health problems living in the community. Health service representatives will need to include sections of the MHA 1983 which are relevant to both admission and discharge arrangements.

While such information may seem self-evident to the agency producing it, it will shed much light on the issue for representatives from other agencies. This process can help to overcome perceptions that, for example, Psychiatrists who do not admit people diagnosed as having 'untreatable' disorders are not merely (or always) being awkward but are operating within the constraints imposed upon them by the Mental Health Act.

The Position Papers can be used to identify shortfalls in the existing systems, and help to concentrate the minds of the steering group on identifying changes in practice which could help to make better use of existing resources.

Questionnaire

A questionnaire which is completed by all the members of the steering group can also help to build up a picture of how much inter-agency collaborative work is already under way. Such a questionnaire can also show everyone in the group just what is really available in terms of hospital beds, day care places and so on (see Appendix II).

Designing a system

The next stage of the process may be fraught with difficulty, for several reasons. Firstly, each agency may have produced its own Position Paper with some satisfaction. Whilst they may feel that their particular papers show how much useful work they are doing, they may be dismayed to discover that colleagues in other agencies think that what they do is in fact not enough.

On the other hand the exercise may reveal information which makes the representatives of some agencies uneasy. It may become apparent that there are major inadequacies and gaps in the services currently available to mentally disordered offenders, for example that there are no day care places available for people with learning disabilities and challenging behaviour.

While those representatives may admit to themselves that their service is not good enough it may be painful, or even impossible for them to admit it to the steering group. They may become defensive and respond by pointing out the gaps in others services. This reaction, although understandable, can be extremely counter-productive to the process of designing a diversion system.

Steering group members need to approach this process in a robust frame of mind, with their minds set clearly on the desired outcome of the process, namely a system that diverts effectively. They must agree not to give in to the temptation to re-enact old battles or rehearse old arguments. The process is about looking forward to something better than that which is available already. It is axiomatic that the problem of mentally disordered offenders is a result partly of the complexity of the interrelationships between the criminal justice process and the caring agencies and partly because of many years of inadequate resourcing of services which provide alternatives to prison.

It can be argued that no one on the steering group needs to feel defensive about what has or has not happened in the past. However, they can afford to be reasonably optimistic about the future. Now is a good time to be designing a diversion system. The climate is right for change and much useful pioneering work has already been done from which groups currently embarking on designing a system can learn.

It is the responsibility of the Chair to take his or her steering group safely through the difficult process of identifying gaps in existing provision, by keeping their minds focused on the desired outcome, namely a system which actually does divert mentally disordered offenders from custody.

Identifying need

When all the Position Papers have been submitted and digested and when the questionnaire has been completed, the steering group will need to turn its attention to assessing need. This is extremely difficult because of the profound differences in approach of each of the agencies which makes any simple counting exercise almost impossible. Because diagnoses vary so widely it is very difficult to calculate how many mentally disordered offenders are in the criminal justice system at any one time.

From a notional group of ten mentally disordered offenders, the police may identify five each week who are arrested for offences and whose condition gives the Custody Officer sufficient cause for concern for him to call out the Forensic Medical Examiner and/or Approved Social Worker, under the provisions of the Police and Criminal Evidence Act 1984. The police may be missing three other people whose symptoms are suppressed by prescribed drugs or who appear to be coping reasonably well with the stresses of arrest and interview.

If all ten individuals were assessed by a Psychiatrist, five might be diagnosed as suffering from a treatable psychiatric illness such as manic depression or schizophrenia, in which case hospital admission may be a possibility. The remaining five may be thought to have untreatable psychopathic disorders or behavioural disorders or even inadequate personalities. If that is the assessment of the Psychiatrist then they may be remanded to custody in which case two of them may be sufficiently obviously disordered to be admitted to the prison or remand centre medical facilities. One of the two may eventually be transferred to a regional secure unit.

This example demonstrates how assessment of need varies according to the perspective of the agency, as well as the skill and training of those who come into contact with the mentally disordered offender. While the police are saying they have five cases each week, there may really be ten. However, the Psychiatrist will say there are four cases and the prison will identify two.

Because of the difficulties highlighted in this example, a consistent method of assessing the number of mentally disordered offenders in the criminal justice system needs to be adopted. There are various methods of assessing need accurately.

Screening in the police station

One method is to arrange for a Psychiatrist/CPN to assess everyone in custody at the busiest local police station twice a day for a month or six weeks. This will give a basic picture of how many mentally disordered offenders are coming into the system. Once the individuals have been identified by the CPN, those cases need to be tracked by the Court probation team, who should keep a record of the outcome for each identified individual.

As well as helping to calculate the numbers involved this process should begin to shed light on where gaps in communication and services exist. If there are sufficient resources it may be possible to continue tracking those individuals who are admitted to hospital, receive out-patient treatment, or are remanded or sentenced to prison.

This identifying and tracking exercise may be able to be carried out within existing resources, for example by seconding a CPN or two or more CPNs on a part-time basis operating a rota.

Once identified and marked in some way the individuals assessed as having some form of mental disorder should be able to be tracked by the probation services own record-keeping system. Court records will have information about outcomes and disposals.

The establishment of a short research project will need clear agreement from all the agencies involved. Systems must be in place, such as attaching a coloured sticker to files, which ensure that cases can be followed. Systems which are agreed and established to facilitate effective assessment of need can form the basis of a Diversion system.

Identifying gaps in services

By reference to the linear diagram, Figure 1.4 (Chapter 1, p. 9) of the criminal justice system, Figure 1.3 (Chapter 1, p. 8) and the chart showing decision-making points of the Criminal Justice System together with the information in 'Key points of intervention', Figure 4.1 (Chapter 4, p. 45) the steering group can work systematically through all the stages of the criminal justice process and complete the chart shown, Figure 6.1 (Chapter 6, p. 66). By identifying what is already being done, and what other resources are needed to take advantage of other opportunities for diversion, the steering group will be beginning the process of designing the ideal diversion system. It may not be possible to achieve all the changes necessary to create the ideal system immediately and it will be a matter for local debate how best to use the limited resources available.

From strategic to operational decision

An idealised design of a scheme is, to all intents and purposes, a strategic vision. The final outcome of turning this into operational practice will depend on many local factors, including the volume of relevant cases going through the local courts, the resources available and the agencies committed to being involved in such an enterprise. Even so, the chart shown in Figure 6.1 can help to bring clarity and focus to that process no matter what the local conditions may be. It provides an opportunity not only to identify the decision making points in the local criminal justice system but also to recognise the work that can be done in between those points to influence the subsequent decision. The purposes of completing the chart Figure 6.1 are:

1. To identify decision makers. As far as the agencies usually involved are concerned there are only three actual decision makers: the police, CPS and the Courts. ASWs and Psychiatrists

can use civil sections of the MHA 1983 to take people out of the system by applying for admission, or admitting them to hospital, but they do not have any other decision making power within it.

2. To provide an easy, visual identification of the areas of involvement of the various agencies and the boundaries to those areas. It should demonstrate very clearly the limited, discrete, yet marginally overlapping domains of the three decision making agencies.
3. To identify the lead agency or agencies in terms of the greatest involvement, either in terms of resource imput or the spread of involvement through the system.
4. To identify which decisions any diversion system should concentrate on influencing, and to avoid spending time considering activities that actually belong in a different stage of the system. It should also highlight the scope for agencies to combine their efforts to increase that influence.
5. To determine which agencies, and which practitioners need to be involved in a particular scheme, and whether the boundaries of any agency's involvement need to be extended.
6. To identify what gaps there are in provision and who needs to address them.
7. To provide a much clearer focus for planning and work, and a focus that can be arrived at more quickly and more easily by using the chart than would otherwise be the case.

If a screening exercise has been carried out at the police station then the steering group will have additional information to that contained in the chart, on which to make decisions about where resources should be concentrated in order to achieve the greatest impact.

The first step in using this chart may be to take the information contained in the Positions Papers and write it into the appropriate squares (the use of 'post-it' notes for this can be very helpful as it allows information to be moved or added to without spoiling the chart). Even at this stage it may become clear that with better communication and better co-operation the existing resources could be used to much better effect.

The 'ideal system' will describe how it wants decision making to change, at least in terms of outcomes. The next step is to identify what activities or systems are most likely to bring about that change. For example, if the targeted decision point is 'CPS consideration' and the preferred outcome is discontinuance, then concentrate on the column between 'Charge' and 'CPS Consideration' and establish who could do what differently that would improve the likelihood of CPS deciding to discontinue proceedings.

Obviously the agencies and practitioners represented on the chart will depend on local conditions and may change if additional resources become available. Another of the benefits of this chart is that it is not static, it can change as circumstances change, as imagination and ideas change and as trust between the agencies grows.

Action to fill the gaps

The police station — training

If the CPN, undertaking a screening exercise in the police station discovers that mentally disordered offenders are frequently not being identified by the Custody Officers, there is one possible step which may be taken immediately to remedy the problem. Additional training may be provided for those responsible.

The Custody Officer has a special responsibility under S38 of PACE if he has reason to believe that a prisoner may be mentally disordered. He must arrange for an Appropriate Adult to be present when the person is interviewed about an alleged offence. He must call out the FME to ensure that the person is fit to be interviewed and an ASW to assess the person's mental health.

None of these safeguards about the health or interests of mentally disordered offenders will be effective, if the Custody Officer fails to recognise that a prisoner is mentally disordered. Training could help Custody Officers to recognise symptoms of mental disorder which may not be immediately obvious. They may then be able to identify types of behaviour which indicate mental disorder. Following recognition, the Custody Officer needs to be able to refer appropriately and receive a quick response from mental health services.

Custody Officers' training costs should be able to be met within force training budgets. If local mental health service trainers can undertake the task it will serve two purposes. Firstly, it will keep the costs of extra training down and secondly it will establish a useful link between the police and the mental health services.

Referral system — from the police station

If the pilot screening exercise showed that one or two mentally disordered offenders were likely to be detained at a particular police station each day it would be worthwhile for the CPN to continue to visit once or twice daily. This will only work *if the CPN or ASW* post specifies these duties and if enough time is allowed for the job to be done thoroughly.

Because the time scales of the criminal justice system are so rigid, the CPN has to be able to respond immediately otherwise a vital opportunity to divert may be lost. It is not practical to expect a CPN or ASW to add visits to the police station to an already full workload. If a mentally disordered offender is identified, action must be taken immediately and the ASW or CPN must be able to follow the case through.

If there is only sufficient ASW/CPN time to visit the police station once each day it should be about 8.00 a.m., after prisoners have been fed but before they are transported to Court. If two visits a day are possible the second visit should be made in mid-afternoon.

If the early visit results in the identification of a mentally disordered offender in the police cells, it may not be possible to do anything other than a quick assessment before he or she is moved to Court. However, the CPN will then be able to alert others about the nature and severity of the problem.

If the screening exercise shows the police station is only likely to have one or two mentally disordered offenders in custody each week then it may be appropriate for the CPN to stop making daily visits and to switch to a referral system. This means that the Custody Officer would be able to call out a CPN or ASW to assess a person giving cause for concern. Clearly this will only work effectively if the Custody Officer has had sufficient training to know when to alert the CPN or ASW, and if the relevant professional is able to respond swiftly to the police referral. Custody time-limits constrain the discretion of the Custody Officer, he therefore needs to be able to contact an ASW or CPN quickly, as soon as a problem is identified and rely on a quick response.

In some areas the police call out the social services emergency duty team, in which case they are competing with every other social work emergency in that area. It is preferable to have a call out system which means that the person in the cells can be assessed in the shortest possible time.

This may be achieved by having a rota of CPNs and ASWs who are on call and who carry a bleep. If four or five professionals were available to make up the rota, the extra work could possibly be absorbed without requiring any additional staffing.

Responsive networks

When a mentally disordered offender has been assessed at the police station and found to be suffering from a sufficiently serious disorder to require admission to hospital there are several ways of achieving this end (see Key points of intervention, Figure 4.1, p. 45). However, all approaches rely on the willingness of the hospital to admit the person.

This is often a very difficult area but it is possible to negotiate working arrangements which facilitate admission from the police station. If the local psychiatric hospital insists on a nursing assessment by ward staff before admission it will be virtually impossible to admit someone directly from the police station unless a nurse is available to do such an assessment round the clock, and at short notice.

It will be very helpful if the ward staff agree to accept the assessment by the rota CPN of the person's mental health and the appropriateness of admission. This will enable the person to be taken to hospital directly from the police station, either as a voluntary patient or under S2 MHA 1983. Admission to hospital at this stage may or may not be the end of the criminal justice process for that individual, depending on the nature of charge, but at least in the meantime he or she can receive skilled care and treatment to alleviate his or her distress.

It may be helpful, and reduce the risk of inappropriate admissions, for a psychiatrist to be available to visit the police station. Most areas have a rota of Psychiatrists who are available for emergency call-outs. If responding to referrals from the police station were included in their duties, it would be immensely helpful to the police, to the CPN or ASW and to the mentally disordered individual.

Identifying gaps in service — at the Magistrates Court

Gaolers

When a mentally disordered offender is taken to Court in custody he or she will be placed in the cells. The gaoler may therefore be the first person to be aware that a particular prisoner is acting or responding in a bizarre way. The Court gaolers therefore need to know to whom to refer such prisoners.

Court probation team

The obvious solution is to refer them to the Court probation team, but does the Court probation team have one or more practitioners with expertise or interest in people who are mentally disordered?

If it does it may be appropriate to extend the role of these particular probation officers and formalise informal arrangements so that all referrals regarding mentally disordered offenders automatically go to them. It may be that only one such person is available. That is clearly better than nothing, but if so, arrangements have to be made to cover that function when that person is absent from work. Referrers need to know to whom to refer and once they get used to that pattern of working it can be very unhelpful to have to remember alternative courses of action to refer when the particular Probation Officer is on leave. Arrangements for cover need to be made in such a way that there is no change to the standing agreement on how to refer mentally disordered offenders. This may mean that if there is only one Probation Officer with expert knowledge, another will need to receive additional training and they will then have to be paired with each other to provide a consistent service throughout the year. The picture will vary form Court to Court depending on the type of area and the volume of cases.

Bail information officer

Is there a Bail Information Officer in the Court? If so, can that person assist the specialist Probation Officers to put together a set of arrangements which make the granting of bail more likely. Will the specialist take responsibility for pre-sentence reports on mentally disordered offenders? Can he or she liaise effectively with the local mental health services to obtain out-patients appointments with Psychiatrists and CPNs?

Psychiatric assessment at Court

Psychiatric assessment at Court may facilitate diversion especially in cases where admission to hospital is not straight forward because there is doubt whether or not the mentally disordered offender is mentally ill, or is treatable under the MHA 1983 These are not the sort of questions which can be answered easily during a quick assessment in the cells, therefore admission under S35 MHA 1983 for up to 28 days for a full assessment may be helpful at the remand stage. It is necessary for a doctor approved under S12 MHA 1983 to provide evidence to the Court that the defendant requires assessment in hospital and that there is a bed available.

If the admission turns out to be inappropriate it is possible for the case to be re-listed, and some other remand disposal sought before the expiry of 28 days. If the admission is useful but 28 days is not long enough, the time may be extended by the Court.

Acute admission wards may be more willing to take a risk and admit under S35 MHA 1983 than they would be to admit under S2 because the discharge from an S35 can be arranged swiftly through the Courts as well as through the usual discharge procedures under the Care Programme Approach which follow an admission under S2 or S3. Admissions from Court under S35 require co-operation from other Psychiatrists and nursing staff on whose wards defendants are admitted by the Court.

This means, in practice, agreeing that a nursing assessment prior to admission is not necessary and that whichever Psychiatrist is at Court, he or she may admit to other wards than his or her own.

It is preferable for the psychiatric assessments at Court to be undertaken by a rota of Psychiatrists rather than by one or two individuals. The number available and willing to take part in the rota will vary from area to area. It will be useful if the rota contains at least one Psychiatrist with special expertise in learning disability, one from forensic psychiatry and one who provides a drugs and alcohol service. As well as bringing their individual expertise to the Court assessment process, they can also be available to give advice and support to their general psychiatry colleagues in appropriate cases.

Admission to hospital

Questions may be asked at this stage about the admission criteria used by the acute admission wards of the local psychiatric hospital. This may be another delicate area of debate but it cannot be avoided. Mental health practitioners may have to justify to their criminal justice agency colleagues why they cannot or will not admit certain types of individuals. The reasons may well be valid, for example the wards may not accept patients requiring some degree of security if it is not physically possible to provide that security.

It can sometimes appear to those outside the mental health services that admission wards can be reluctant to admit anyone whose behaviour is at all challenging, or that swift discharge is sometimes arranged for individuals who are still not fit to be discharged, but who have become troublesome.

While mental health workers may argue rightly that hospital wards cannot be used as a dustbin into which any defendant who is behaving oddly is put, they will need to confirm for themselves by discussion with colleagues in other agencies that they have got the balance between accepting and refusing admission about right.

They may also need to ask themselves if they respond quickly enough. If services are not available when and where they are needed then those who desperately need them *will* not be able to use them. If admission from Court is not possible then the defendant may well be remanded to prison where he or she may wait for weeks to be seen by a Psychiatrist who then may admit to hospital. The intervening weeks in prison may have caused the defendant's mental health to deteriorate still further, resulting in a much more intractable problem for the hospital staff on admission, as well as weeks of unnecessary distress for the individual.

Therefore it may be in the interests of the mental health practitioners to provide a responsive flexible service to the Courts to help prevent inappropriate remands in custody for psychiatric reports.

4 Key points of intervention

The police station — arrest

When arresting a mentally disordered offender in a public place for an offence, the police officer may have a choice either to detain under the provisions of S136 MHA 1983 or to arrest for the offence itself. In theory that choice should be made at the time of arrest and be irrevocable. However, in practice the situation is rarely so clear cut. Sometimes an officer may arrest a person for an offence and then realise that the prisoner has a mental health problem, or a learning disability. At that point the officer may decide, if the offence is not serious, to use his/her powers under S136 to remove the person to a 'place of safety'.

The 'place of safety' can be a hospital or a police station. If it is the police station the situation may change again. If for example a person who has committed a minor public order offence is taken into custody under S136, he or she will not be cautioned as would have been the case following arrest for an offence. However, if on the journey to the police station, the person talks to the officer about having committed another more serious offence, for example 'I was upset because I can't go home, I set fire to my flat', he may then be arrested for arson and then cautioned.

Thus, although his destination has not changed and he is still going to the police station, his status has changed profoundly. He is no longer in police custody for his own safety, under a time-limited section of the MHA 1983, he is now about to be sucked into a criminal justice process, which if uninterrupted could result in his being sentenced to prison for life or spending many years in a secure hospital.

This example shows that decisions made by police officers before or after arrest can make a crucial difference to the eventual outcome for the mentally disordered offender.

Decision Maker	Decision Making Point		Choices
Officer in Case	i) Arrest		:For criminal offence or S136 MHA 1983
		or	:Alert and deliver into charge of caring agency
Custody Sgt.	ii) Detention		:For determining sufficiency of evidence to charge S37 (1)PACE For securing/preserving evidence S37(2) PACE (including interview with appropriate adult) For charging or bailing S37(7) PACE
		or	:Bail to return to police station
Custody Sgt.	iii) Charge		:Detain to identify/protect defendant; prevent physical injury/loss/damage by defendant; prevent absconscion or interference with administration of justice or investigation S38(1) PACE
		or	:Bail to Court
CPS/Court	iv) Remand		:Remand in custody to prevent absconcion, further offending, interference with witnesses/investigation; for protection of defendant. Bail Act 1976, Sched. 1 Part 1.
		or	:Bail to return to court
		or	:Remand to hospital for report S35 MHA 1983
		or	:(Crown Court) remand to hospital for treatment S36
Home Office		or	:Removal to hospital for treatment S48
Court	v) Sentence		:Custodial Sentence
		or	:Committed to hospital for sentence S44 MHA 1983 awaiting restriction order
		or	:Interim hospital order S38
		or	:Hospital order S37
Home Office		or	:Removal to hospital after conviction S47
		or	:Alternative disposal

Figure 4.1 Key points of intervention

Caution

If a person with a mental health problem or learning disability is arrested for a minor offence, the police may decide to take no further action and release the person with an informal warning. If the offence is admitted they may decide to administer a caution which is recorded, and then take no further action. However, if someone appears very distressed or confused, or is behaving in a violent or aggressive way in the police station, the police may be reluctant to take no further action or to caution, if this results in the person being released with no one to take care of him or her, and a strong likelihood that he or she will re-offend, or else come to some harm.

Charge

In such cases the tendency is to charge with an offence, keep the person in custody overnight and dispatch the person, and the responsibility for decision making and disposal to the Magistrates Court in the morning. If the person is evidently disordered in the cells the Custody Officer must send for the Forensic Medical Examiner (FME) to say whether the person is fit to be detained and questioned. However, not all FMEs are S12 MHA 1983 approved doctors and may therefore fail to diagnose mental disorder.

Once a person has been charged he or she may be bailed from the police station, under the PACE Act 1984, to return to the police station later. Bail may also be allowed after arrest, but before a charge is made if further enquiries still have to be made.

Discontinuance

At any point between charge and trial the CPS may be asked by the defence to exercise its right to discontinue proceedings. The Code for Crown Prosecutors established the principle that prosecution will not be appropriate when the accused person was suffering from a mental disorder at the time the offence was committed, unless prosecution is in the public interest. Whether or not the prosecution is discontinued will be influenced by factors such as the gravity of the offence, the nature of the mental disorder, and the availability of alternatives to custody.

Public Interest Case Assessment

The code for Crown Prosecutors directs that a prosecutor must be satisfied not only that the evidence in a case presents a realistic prospect of conviction but also that the public interest requires a prosecution. The Code lists public interest criteria which relate to issues of public policy as well as to the individual circumstances of the defendant and the offence. Prosecutors are asked to give careful consideration to the discontinuing prosecutions of various categories of defendant, including people with mental illness whose condition may be worsened by the strain of criminal proceedings.

In order to carry out reviews of a case to judge whether or not it is in the public interest to prosecute, the CPS requires relevant, accurate and verified information about the mentally disordered offender's personal circumstances. This information needs to be provided in such a form that it relates to the criteria in the Code, so that a speedy and effective review can be made of the case. However, the CPS is not able to collect such information directly. In some case, information may be available from the police, but they may only have access to unverified and partial information.

Public Interest Case Assessment helps to bridge this gap and provide the Prosecutor with the information needed to decide whether or not it is in the public interest to prosecute a particular individual. Various PICA schemes have been piloted since the first pilot study was carried out in 1988. PICA schemes work by contacting the defendant and offering the opportunity for an interview. The initial contact letter will make it clear that there is no guarantee that participating in the interview will lead to discontinuance. The defendants are then interviewed by a probation officer and asked questions about their personal situation. The interview will cover the defendant's domestic situation, health, financial circumstances and contact with other agencies.

The interviewer cannot discuss the circumstances surrounding the alleged offence. The purpose of the interview is to elicit information which will help the prosecutor decide the issue of public interest in the case. Information obtained must be verified before it is passed onto the CPS in an agreed form. The interviewer does not make a recommendation, the decision whether or not to discontinue remains entirely with the prosecutor.

It may be possible to incorporate a PICA type scheme into a system of diversion for mentally disordered offenders. The interview could be conducted by a specialist probation officer or by another appropriate professional, by agreement with the CPS. What is important is that the information is verified and that it addresses the issues which are relevant to the CPS process of reviewing public interest in prosecutions (see Appendix III).

Magistrates Court

Remand

At the first appearance in Court the issue of whether or not bail should be granted will be settled within the terms of the Bail Act 1976. There is a presumption under the Bail Act that all defendants including those with mental disorders are entitled to bail unless there is a risk of absconsion, of further offending, interference with witnesses or the investigation of the offence. A remand in custody may also be made for the protection of the defendant. The CPS solicitor in the magistrates court may oppose an application for bail on behalf of the mentally disordered defendant, on the ground that the defendant is likely to run away, commit further offences or come to some harm. These points are often used to argue for a refusal of bail to mentally disordered persons.

If the defendant is granted bail it may be with conditions, for example that he or she resides at a particular address, possibly a hospital ward. This may often be the only way of arranging the admission to hospital from Court, in the absence of a psychiatrist or if the condition of the defendant is not sufficiently severe to warrant detention in hospital under a civil section of the MHA 1983.

If the defendant has been committed for trial to the Crown Court he or she may be remanded to hospital under S36 MHA 1983 for treatment.

If a psychiatrist is available at Court, the defendant may be admitted to hospital from Court for an assessment and for a report to Court to be undertaken, under S35 MHA 1983.

Conviction

If the defendant is found guilty and if the offence is sufficiently serious, a custodial sentence may be made. If convicted in the Magistrates Court, he or she may then be committed to the Crown Court under S48 MHA 1983 in order that the Court may impose a hospital order with restriction, under the terms of S41 MHA 1983.

Following conviction, an interim hospital order or a hospital order may be made under S38, or S37 MHA respectively. Restrictions may be imposed under S41 MHA 1983 either with or without time limits. S41 has the effect of placing complete control on whether a person may leave hospital on where he or she lives and whether he or she is discharged from hospital.

Following conviction, if a person is sentenced to custody but is in need of hospital treatment for a mental disorder, he or she may be transferred from prison to hospital under S47 MHA 1983. Where the defendant has been committed to the Crown Court he or she may be remanded to hospital under S36 MHA 1983. Where the defendant is remanded in custody from prison to hospital under S48 MHA 1983, a transfer, if he or she is suffering from a mental illness or severe impairment which requires treatment, may be appropriate. In the case of a psychopathic disorder, or mental impairment such a transfer will only be allowed, if treatment is likely to alleviate the condition or prevent a deterioration.

This limitation makes transfer dependant on the opinion of two Psychiatrists that a psychopathic disorder or mental impairment is amenable to treatment. The issue of treatability is therefore crucial to the success of any attempt to transfer a person from prison to hospital. It is possible for a defendant to obtain an independent psychiatric report on the issue of treatability.

Remand in custody — Transfer S48

If it becomes apparent that the defendant is likely to be remanded in custody, the defence solicitor can ask for a short remand and those operating the Diversion system can use the intervening days to make whatever arrangements, such as supported housing, out-patient appointments and assesments reports and so-on as are likely to make remand on bail an acceptable alternative to the Magistrates at the next appearance.

If security, rather than social support or housing is the real issue, the problem becomes more difficult to solve because of the national shortage of low and medium secure hospital beds.

A psychiatric assessment will be needed to examine the issue of risk and dangerousness. This is a difficult area as there are no uniformly applied standards by which risk may be measured. The Courts will, quite rightly err on the side of caution. Therefore a remand in custody may be inevitable until a secure hospital bed can be arranged.

Transfers from prison to hospital for prisoners on remand are arranged under S48 of MHA 1983 or S47, in the case of a convicted person, by order of the Home Secretary. First, the defendant must be assessed and a hospital bed found which is suitable in terms of treatment needs and security. Timescales for admission will then be agreed, authorisation must be sought from C3 Division of the Home Office.

This process can take a long time to complete. Delay can be caused by a failure by the prison medical staff to recognise the presence of mental disorder. Then the prisoner will usually be assessed by a Psychiatrist from his home health authority who may find it difficult to arrange a visit to the prison or remand centre to carry out the assessment.

Unless the home health authority has a suitable facility, admission to hospital in the prisoner's home area may not be agreed and a placement outside his home health authority will be sought.

(i) The prison medical staff may then seek admission to a secure hospital, Rampton, Ashworth or Broadmoor.

Contrary to popular belief it is not easy to get into a secure hospital. It is however remarkably difficult to get out of one. Once admitted to a secure hospital via the criminal justice system, a patient is likely to stay there for about six to eight years. If the patient makes some recovery before that time has elapsed, it may be difficult for the Special Hospital to discharge patients directly to the community. For many the preferred route is via a medium secure unit or a local psychiatric hospital in their home area which can prepare them for re-integration into society. Therefore if a mentally disordered defendant is pleading not guilty to a serious charge, or is charged with an offence which is not likely to carry a long custodial sentence, admission to a secure hospital while on remand is not an attractive option. However, the prisoner may be very disturbed and confused, and his Solicitor may not be experienced in dealing with mentally disordered clients. There is no easy way for a Defence Solicitor to liaise with prison medical staff or to advocate on behalf of his or her client to ensure that an admission to a secure hospital in not sought for someone whose best interests may actually be served by remaining in prison. Because they are mental hospitals, secure hospitals will use the test of 'treatability' before detaining anyone with a psychopathic or personality disorder. Therefore, the Special Hospitals cannot provide a service for someone with an intractable personality disorder if the hospital medical staff do not think it is treatable.

Any diversion system should include arrangements for facilitating transfers when they are appropriate. However, this will require the co-operation of the Prison Medical Officer and the probation team in the prison or remand centre.

(ii) Regional Secure Units

The Regional Secure Unit may be a more attractive solution. Firstly the environment of Regional Secure Units tends to be better than older parts of the Special Hospitals. Most of them were built in the late 1970s and 1980s on an acceptable scale. However, this may mean they have less space for recreation than the Special Hospitals. The regime in RSUs tends to be more testing of the individual than that of a Special Hospital.

They are unfortunately frequently full, and operate a waiting list system. The usual length of stay is about two years, during which time the treatment and rehabilitation offered is geared to enabling the person to be returned to the community safely. Because they are so over-subscribed and because their service is geared to those likely to respond to intensive treatment and rehabilitation within the expected two year period regional Secure Units can afford to be choosy about whom they admit.

They will be more favourably disposed to admission for people with mental health problems which respond well to treatment. They may well refuse to admit someone with whom they do not feel they can make significant progress in the two-year period.

The role of C3 division

The process of transfer under S48 may be very slow but it can actually be arranged with remarkable speed and efficiency by C3, provided that they are asked to do so. Transfers can be arranged within two hours, provided they receive medical evidence that it is necessary and appropriate, and a bed is available.

Why then do so many mentally disordered offenders languish in prison for weeks or months, either on remand or following sentence, awaiting a transfer? The answer could be one, or a combination of a number of factors. The transfer system relies on prison medical staff being quick to respond to the needs of mentally disordered offenders. It also relies on co-operation and a swift repsonse from psychiatrists in other areas, on the relevant paperwork being completed and a suitable bed being available.

The problem of transfers, can therefore be difficult to address. However, C3 is a useful resource for solving these difficulties and is very willing to offer advice, if asked. The number of transfers arranged by C3 Division has risen dramatically in recent years from under 100 in 1986 to over 700 in 1993, of whom only a small proportion, 60 or so have gone to Special Hospitals.

Sentencing

(i) *Options*

If the mentally disordered offender is found guilty of the offence, he or she may be sentenced in the Magistrates Court or committed to the Crown Court for sentence. If the offence is not serious or the mentally disordered offender can be offered a suitable package of care arranged as part of a Diversion system the Court is inclined to use a non-custodial sentence, such as an absolute or conditional discharge.

A probation order is also a possible alternative to custody, although someone with severe mental health problems or a learning disability may have difficulty in complying with a probation order. Someone who has a chaotic life, or who is very confused by his or her condition or disabled by psychiatric medication may find it impossible to keep appointments. A person whose condition makes it difficult for him or her to accept reality will present serious problems for a probation officer trying to work with the client to confront the issues which lead to the offending and explore opportunities for change.

However, for some mentally disordered offenders, a probation order may be a useful starting point for constructing their lives with skilled professional support. It would be useful if at least one member of every probation field team had sufficient training in order to be able to deal effectively with clients with mental health problems. However, it is unreasonable and unrealistic to expect even the most experienced and skilled Probation Officer to be able to provide an effective service alone. A probation order should be part of a complete package of care, including psychiatric support, housing, day care and social support as appropriate.

A suspended sentence may be useful if the mentally disordered offender has sufficient insight and understanding to appreciate that a repetition of the offending behaviour may lead to a custodial sentence being imposed. This disposal needs to be linked with an effective package of care if it is to achieve the desired aim and prevent re-offending.

(ii) Pre-sentence reports

When considering sentencing a mentally disordered offender the Court should have a pre-sentence report completed by a Probation Officer. This should review the offending history, the person's mental health at the time of the offence, and at the time of sentence. The pre-sentence report could also highlight the disposal which the Probation Officer thinks will be most effective.

(iii) Psychiatric reports

A psychiatric report may be completed by a psychiatrist who is part of a Court assessment scheme and to whom the mentally disordered offender was referred on first or second appearance in the Magistrates Court.

A person may also have been remanded to hospital under S35 for assessment and the Court will receive a psychiatric report based on that assessment. A psychiatric report may have been completed while the defendant is on remand, either as an outpatient on bail, or while on remand in custody, in prison.

The court may order a psychiatric report to be made, as may the defence. It is usually possible for legally-aided defendants to arrange an independent psychiatric report which does not have to be disclosed to the prosecution if it is unhelpful for the defendant's case.

If the prosecution commission a psychiatric report, the CPS may disclose it to the defence. In addition to requesting psychiatric reports to inform sentencing decisions, the CPS may wish to have a psychiatric report before agreeing to discontinue proceedings, in order to be sure that the defendant really is mentally disordered within the meaning of the Mental Health Act 1983 and is not merely suffering from stress brought on by being caught.

5 The role of the prison

Introduction

Agencies which have responsibilities to provide services in the community are largely relieved of those responsibilities when a person who is mentally disordered is remanded or sentenced to prison.

The prison is outside the usual working arrangements which enable agencies in the community to co-operate to provide community care. The prison may be outside the town or city it serves, standing in forbidding isolation amidst ploughed fields. Even if it is within the town or city, its high walls and punitive architecture serve to prevent it being an integrated part of the local society.

The isolation of the prison has been exacerbated in the past by the self-sufficiency of the prison service, which makes its own towels and grows its own vegetables. There was, until recently, little need to have much contact with the outside world. It is as if in our midst, prisoners and people who work in the prison service are exiles in their own country.

The barriers which created that exile situation are gradually being broken down. Privatisation and market testing of prisons, contracting out of parts of the work of prisons, devolution of purchasing budgets to individual establishments, have all contributed to a gradual erosion of the fortress-like isolation of the prison service. While there are many who would argue that these changes are morally or economically indefensible, it is not the purpose of this chapter to make judgements but to sketch the picture, as it is, not as it perhaps should be. A broad understanding of the process and progress of change within the prison system will inform consideration of opportunities for further development and change which may be of benefit to mentally disordered offenders.

Prison health care

As part of this larger pattern of change, changes have also taken place in the prison medical service, and in the way in which the prison provides for the health and social care needs of its inmates.

Devolution of health care budgets may enable the prison to create a mixed economy of care where some aspects of health care for mentally disordered offenders continue to be provided by prison medical and nursing staff, while other needs are met by services purchased elsewhere.

Although health commissioning by prisons is not yet widespread it provides an opportunity for the prisons to become stakeholders in the purchasing of local services and increases the chances of a better service for mentally disordered offenders in prisons. Joint commissioning also helps to emphasise that prisoners are not 'elsewhere' or in exile, they are here, and along with the rest of the population require good quality and comprehensive services to meet their individual needs. If the prison contributes to the cost of providing a Forensic Psychiatrist in the community it will be entitled to demand the same standard of care for its inmates as they would have had had they been in the community.

Mentally disordered offenders in prison

Introduction

Diversion from custody systems, if they were in effective operation throughout the country, would dramatically reduce the number of mentally disordered offenders remanded or sentenced to custody. The independent evaluation of the North Humberside Project undertaken by Drs Midgely and Cohen at the Centre for System Studies at the University of Hull, showed a diversion rate of 85 per cent in the first full year of operation. However, there is always likely to be a small residual prison population of mentally disordered offenders, for a number of reasons. Therefore the prison will have to continue to make some provision to meet their needs, as their numbers decline. A substantial reduction in the number of mentally disordered offenders in the prison should make it easier for the prison to meet the needs of those remaining.

Prisoners with less serious mental illness and learning disability

Where efforts to divert mentally disordered offenders have failed or are not appropriate (see Mental health offending matrix Figures 1.1 and 1.2, Chapter 1, p. 4) the prison becomes responsible for the care of prisoners who have less serious problems. Transfer to hospital will not be necessary but such prisoners are nevertheless very vulnerable by comparison with the majority of the prison population. Vulnerable prisoner units may be able to provide an adequate level of care and support for mentally ill or learning disabled prisoners. However, places may not always be available. Such units have prisoners who are vulnerable to attack within the prison system because of the nature of their crimes. The mentally disordered offender may therefore not fit in with the rest of the vulnerable prisoner unit population and be as isolated and threatened as they would have been in a normal location within the prison system. When in the community such individuals may be able to access a range of caring and support services including contact with a CPN, a key worker, out-patient visits to a Psychiatrist, attendance at a day centre, run by social services or a voluntary organisation such as MIND.

In the prison these services are not available. The only social care agency which operates within the prison is Probation. Due to the high ratio of prisoners to Probation Officers, the probation service within the prison may have a very limited role. It cannot be all things to all inmates although it is often expected to undertake a wide variety of work such as responsibility for prisoners' welfare and working with prisoners to confront offending behaviour. The prison probation service with its existing establishment cannot provide a comprehensive social support service for mentally disordered offenders. It could be argued that prison officers should contribute to the provision of services to meet the welfare and social care needs of prisoners. Some prison officers do attempt to fill this role, for example in establishments and units which have a personal officer system. However, it is difficult to combine a caring role with a custodial function. There are also many other demands on a prison officer's time.

It could be argued that the service should be expanded to fill this gap, but this would re-enforce the tendency to see the problem as one which could be solved by one agency alone. Such a solution would also lead to the prison being seen as an acceptable destination for mentally disordered offenders.

Should the prison provide such services and mirror the range of care and support services provided in the community? This is a real dilemma for the Prison Service. They seem already to operate as emergency substitutes for bail hostel, mental hospitals and de-toxification units.

Would, therefore, the provision of a wider range of social care services for mentally disordered offenders within the prison exacerbate an existing tendency to use the prisons as a dumping ground. If the prison could provide an acceptable substitute for care in the community, would it be swamped by a sudden influx of inmates who would previously have been diverted in order to receive those services in the community.

This does not solve the problems of those who do end up in prison and who still need health and social care maintenance.

One way in which the prison can resolve this dilemma is to become involved with all the local agencies in solving local problems relating to mentally disordered offenders.

The membership of a Governor from a local prison or remand centre of the local steering group is crucial to this process. The steering group can act as a forum for discussing how best to meet the needs of those prisoners who have health and social care needs which cannot be met fully by resources available in the prison. The prison can provide daily work, basic education and social skills training. It can invite voluntary organisations in to operate within the prison for example the Samaritans and MIND, and agencies which work with drug abusers.

Joint commissioning with health and social services of some additional responsive services should help the prison to meet the individual needs of prisoners who cannot be diverted for any reason without creating a system of care which would encourage sentencers and others to feel that prison is a good way of accessing services for this group.

Prisoners with untreatable personality or psychopathic disorders

This group has been a cause of considerable concern for some time. The label 'psychopath' may be applied to a mentally disordered offender very loosely by a Psychiatrist but there is no universally applied test for psychopathy. The diagnostic features usually applied to people with psychopathic disorders include coldness, absence of guilt, impulsivity and an inability to control anger. However, diagnoses will still rely on the subjective view of the Psychiatrist which may be incorrect. Such an incorrect diagnosis may have serious long-term consequences for a mentally disordered offender. It is not unheard of for a person who has been subject to compulsory treatment under the MHA 1983 for a mental illness to have their diagnosis changed to one of personality disorder when their behaviour becomes more challenging. The change of diagnosis has the effect of denying further hospital treatment because hospitals are usually very reluctant to admit those labelled psychopaths. The issue of treatability is very significant because under the terms of the MHA 1983 persons with a psychopathic disorder may only be detained for treatment if their disorder is deemed to be treatable.

The reason for this exclusion is understandable. It is not morally right to detain a person for treatment from which by the very nature of their disorder they cannot benefit. Also it is a prerequisite of the success of any behavioural treatment that the mentally disordered offender is willing and able to engage in assessment and treatment and to identify and explore the causes of aggressive and offending behaviour. However, because there are no objective tests for 'treatability' or 'personality disorder' a person who may have benefited from treatment or rehabilitation will be denied access to mental health services because a particular label has been applied to them on the basis of one psychiatric opinion.

It is therefore likely that mentally disordered offenders who are labelled untreatable psychopaths will be remanded and sentenced to custody. Some psychopathic personalities may respond well to the discipline and structure of prison. Others may be outwardly conforming and so not present a visible management problem. However, prisoners with challenging behaviour present enormous management problems to the prison service. Although politicians may argue that prison works because it removes dangerous psychopaths from the streets, it should not be forgotten that such people may continue to commit crimes within the prison system. Their victims will be prison officers and other prisoners. They will eventually be released. The problem is thus contained and delayed but not solved.

Prison discipline works largely by consent. Most prisoners comply reasonably well with prison regulations. If all prisoners presented challenging behaviour the prison system would not be able to function. The only way in which prison systems can respond to challenging behaviour, regardless of its cause, is with punishment. Punishment merely reinforces the normality of the challenging behaviour, without confronting the cause or offering incentives to change. Mentally disordered offenders with psychopathic disorders may spend long periods in solitary confinement in segregation units, because their behaviour is too challenging to be managed on normal location within the prison.

The prison system provides very little positive input for this type of mentally disordered offender. A few places may be available in special units within the prison system. Such units are, however, the subject of some controversy within the prison system. Some would say that because the conditions in such units are usually better than in other parts of the prison, the system is actually rewarding bad behaviour by sending people with psychopathic disorders to them.

Others would argue that special units reward improvements in behaviour. Prisoners have to be selected for such units and may be deselected if they do not maintain an acceptable standard of behaviour.

By providing intensive support for such prisoners, special units may succeed where all else has failed. The facilities available in special units may enable prisoners to channel their energy into something creative rather than destructive.

Grendon Underwood provides a therapeutic regime for violent offenders. The aim of the regime is to challenge the violent offender to make him think about, and take responsibility for, the consequences of his violence. The regime is, therefore, very difficult for some prisoners with psychopathic disorders to cope with. Ultimately, if the prisoner is not able to adapt to the more demanding regime at Grendon Underwood they may be deselected and returned to an ordinary prison.

Although there may be opportunities within special units and HMP Grendon Underwood to provide a more constructive response to psychopathic disorder, the problem remains and has to be contained and managed by the prison service somewhere within one of its establishments. Thus the most challenging prisoners tend to be moved frequently in order to share the burden and ease tensions. The also carry with them a sense of failure, especially if they are selected and then deselected for a special unit. The only way in which the prison service can be relieved of responsibility is for a S47 transfer to be arranged to a special hospital (see Chapter 6).

Prisoners awaiting transfer

When prisoners are assessed in prison as suffering from a form of mental disorder which is treatable under the MHA 1983, arrangements will be made to transfer them to a suitable hospital.

This process may be slow if it relies on visits to the prison of more than one Psychiatrist or if there is uncertainty about the appropriate level of security. Even after these matters have been settled satisfactorily there may still be no bed available in the hospital to which the prisoner is to be transferred, in which case he or she may have to wait for several weeks in prison until the transfer can be completed, during which time he or she may deteriorate. He may not have access to a qualified Psychiatrist and the standard of facilities and nursing care provided in the prison health care centre is likely to be inadequate. In addition he may only be given such treatment as he consents to because the provisions of the MHA 1983 which permit compulsory treatment do not apply to prison hospitals.

After transfer to hospital and subsequent treatment, the condition of the mentally disordered offender may improve considerably.

The hospital may then decide he is sufficiently well to return to prison. However, on return, unless he consents to continue his medication, he may well deteriorate again. Major tranquillisers are usually prescribed for psychotic conditions. They can have very unpleasant side effects, especially if a higher than recommended dose is prescribed. People with psychotic symptoms may chose to live with the distressing symptoms of their condition rather than take major tranquillisers. However, if this results in a deterioration of their condition they may not be able to cope in prison and may have to be transferred to hospital again.

Prevention of re-offending

The role of the prison in society is, broadly speaking, to punish and deter. However, the high rate of reconviction suggests it is not successful in performing this function for the majority of offenders. The prison system is especially ill-equipped to punish and deter mentally disordered offenders for a number of reasons.

Some mentally disordered offenders want to be in prison because they feel safer in a highly structured environment. This may be because they have spent all their lives in institutions such as children's homes and mental or learning disability hospitals, and they therefore feel at home in prison. It may also be because they are so disabled by their mental disorder that the prison, which provides at least the rudiments of existence and demands very little in return, seems a safe haven in a confusing and frightening world.

People who have suffered from serious mental ill health or learning disability may not be able to weigh the risks involved in committing an offence before they do so. The deterrent effect of prison will only be operated if the mentally disordered offender does not wish to go to prison and realises that a custodial remand or sentence will follow the offence.

The limited work which the prison service does currently undertake with prisoners to help re-offending is geared to helping those who can cope with everyday life and who have a reasonable chance of employment, rather than those with additional problems, such as mentally disordered offenders.

This highlights the importance of diversion from custody for mentally disordered offenders. If it is impossible to work to prevent re-offending within the prison system, it is essential that mentally disordered offenders do not get into the prison system. Breaking the cycle of offending for mentally disordered offenders has to be done outside the prison in order to help prevent them returning to the criminal justice systems and prison.

People with mental health problems who offend and who do serve custodial sentences are often released with nothing other than a set of clothes, a small sum of money and the address of a hostel for the homeless. This is particularly true of people who serve less than twelve months. They will be released without any supervision, unless they specifically ask for it. It is hardly surprising that many re-offend. The probation service within the prison will do what it can to make suitable arrangements. Some prisoners are very hard to place and require a high level of support. Probation recommend that certain services are available for a mentally disordered offender on release but they cannot ensure those services are delivered.

One of the aims of an effective diversion system should be to provide such people with all the support they need as soon as they are released to prevent relapse and re-offending.

A community care assessment and care programme where appropriate are crucial to the creation of a complete package of support for a mentally disordered offender on release from prison. However, such assessments are not carried out before the person leaves prison (see Gordon, 1993 Cheston, 1993 and Miles, 1993).

Therefore, even if there is not a long waiting period for an assessment, it may well be some weeks after release before the person is assessed. This problem may be exacerbated if the person leaves whatever temporary accommodation was found for him and is lost sight of.

Community care assessments should be undertaken in prison for all mentally disordered prisoners, allowing a sufficient time before the end of their sentence to allow arrangements to be made for housing, social support and medical care to enable the person to cope on release and to help prevent further re-offending. A pilot project in Wessex has shown how effective such pre-release arrangements can be.

On release most mentally disordered offenders will be able to be cared for in the community. Some may have homes to go to, others could go into residential homes or specialist supported housing. However, there is a national shortage of good quality supported housing for people with mental health problems. Offenders will be competing for this limited space with those discharged from hospital who have not offended. A 'forensic' label can often deter housing providers from offering accommodation to mentally disordered offenders.

Private residential homes may provide an adequate level of care for mentally disordered offenders who are not able to manage to look after themselves. However many provide a very poor environment, which is restrictive and unstimulating. They do not provide a satisfactory long-term solution for most mentally disordered offenders.

Access to them is via the community care assessment system so even if a person wished to live in such an environment the cost would only be met by social services if the assessment showed the person as needing that level of care. The social services department is not obliged to pay for forms of housing which provide a lower level of support. One possible function of a local multi-agency diversion steering group would be to assess the need for specialist supported housing in its area. The funding of such supported housing is Byzantine in its complexity (Louise Villeneuve, 1993). However, it may be possible to obtain sufficient funding from a variety of sources to establish a hostel for mentally disordered offenders on release in order to provide them with the housing and care they require in order not to re-offend.

6 Diversion into what?

Introduction

In the initial enthusiasm of seeking to get things done, of trying to avoid having so many mentally disordered people languishing in prison cells, the question 'diversion into what?' may seem like something of a side issue. However, it is vital to consider this question and its implications in order to secure the success of any diversion project in terms of influencing decisions, safeguarding individual mentally disordered offenders and protecting the public. Four basic questions must be asked: First, 'why bother about it?' — why it has to be worth it; secondly, 'Who needs what?' — the issues about a differential response to individual need; thirdly, 'Whose responsibility?' — who is charged and funded to respond to need and where are the gaps; and lastly, 'What can be done with inadequate provision?' — the challenge for everyone working in this field. Obviously there are some implicit assumptions in this sequence of questions but hopefully they will be justified during the course of this chapter.

Why bother about it?

Essentially the response to this question comes in two distinct but linked parts, each of which will be of considerable importance to anyone involved in planning or operating a diversion scheme; it should not be thought that one part is more important than the other. First it is important in order to establish the confidence of decision makers. If we start from the premise that the principal decision makers in this process (i.e. the Police, the Crown Prosecution Service and the Courts) do not resort to the use of custody out of a malicious desire to be gratuitously unpleasant to mentally disordered offenders, then we have to conclude that they will want to make use of other options if they are presented. However, custody does tend to promote confidence on two fronts. Firstly, members of the public are not at risk during this period and secondly that the individual prisoner will at least be fed and sheltered. Any other options offered will have to address these two issues for a decision-maker to feel confident enough to choose them instead of custody. Consequently, except in the most minor of cases, it is not enough to make the case that an accused person is a mentally disordered offender, the case has to be made that this person will have the appropriate resources available to them (e.g. accommodation, day care, CPN/GP involvement).

The second reason for bothering comes from caring about the individual caught up in the criminal justice system. Although the drive behind the establishment of diversion schemes is the desire not to have people needlessly held in custody, this on its own is something of a negative aim. It is important that there is also an ambition to see people responded to appropriately at a local level; this is the demonstration of the positive side of that aim. In the midst of this, however, we need to retain a sense of balance, to keep an eye on protecting the individual's rights as well as trying to ensure that they get what professionals think they need. The 1983 Mental Health Act goes to considerable lengths to enshrine individual rights and established formal structures to make sure that policy is turned into practice. This was as a response to the almost unfettered discretion afforded under the 1959 Act so we need to take care not to undermine what was a very laudable intention indeed. That it is quite easy for a person who has attracted attention through the commission of an offence to spend longer in conditions of some security on the grounds of treatment than they ever would have done as a punishment.

Who needs what?

Inevitably, finding the appropriate response for any individual is enormously complex and depends on a variety of factors. Unfortunately, to some extent, in addition to the many individual factors, it may also depend on what stage a particular person has reached in the criminal justice process, for example the package of care required to persuade the police to take no further action could almost certainly be much simpler than that required to persuade a Court not to resort to custody.

Although in taking an overview of the practicalities of setting up a new scheme it is inevitable, to some extent, that a simplistic approach has to be adopted to categorising the likely population being considered, it is nonetheless vital to bear in mind the message conveyed in an article by Jean Collins (1993):

> There is a tendency to classify people who have similar 'needs' and wishes together, and to expect that those superficial similarities identify them as ideal house or flat-mates.

This point is included at this stage because it is important to acknowledge that above all, we are working with individuals and, although what follows, of necessity, categorises on the basis of superficial similarity, in practice all these considerations need to be individualised.

The first part of this superficial categorisation rests on the balance between the seriousness of the offence or alleged offence and the seriousness of the mental disorder. The matrix that demonstrates that balance (see Figure 6.1) is not intended to suggest an absolute rule but a guide to the areas to be considered. In simple terms, the areas considered in this diagram come under three broad headings: accommodation, treatment/support and criminal justice disposals.

Accommodation

An individual's accommodation needs are primarily determined by their social circumstances, including the seriousness of the mental disorder. It has to be acknowledged, however, that the Courts may decide that, to some extent, the degree of security of that accommodation is determined by the seriousness of the offence as well. This means that a great variety of types of accommodation will need to be accessible locally to respond to the myriad combinations of seriousness that will be thrown up. These will range from independent facilities such as the family home, council or privately rented accommodation to lodgings, supported lodgings and hostels. The type of hostel required will depend on the level and nature of help needed from staff (e.g. general hostel such as YMCA or Salvation Army, or specialist mental health or learning disability hostels such as those run by Housing Associations, MIND, MENCAP or Richmond Fellowship or a hostel for offenders such as Stonham or Probation).

Treatment/support

Obviously the first step in identifying treatment/support needs and responding to them is an assessment. Depending on the circumstances (including the current involvement or otherwise of one of the relevant agencies) this initial assessment could be undertaken by the GP, an ASW, a CPN or a Psychiatrist. The kind of provision that will be needed to respond to the variety of needs will have to range from the supportive home visits of CPNs, GP treatment, day centre and day-care facilities, local hospital facilities

Seriousness of offence			
HIGH	Hostel, residential home, own accomm. GP, CPN support. Probation, Probation + condition (res, treatment), CSO.	Hospital, RSU, hostel. GP, CPN support, day-care facility, out-patient treatment Probation + condition. Hospital Order.	RSU, hospital, Special Hospital. In patient treatment Hospital Order.
MEDIUM	Hostel, residential home, own accomm. GP, CPN support. Probation, CSO, cond. disch.	Hostel, residential home. Day-care facility, GP, CPN support, out-patient treatment. Probation, cond discharge.	Hospital, hostel. In/out patient treatment, GP, CPN support, day-care facility. Probation +condition hospital order.
LOW	Own accomm., lodgings, hostel. GP, CPN support. Cond disch., fine.	Own accomm. lodgings, hostel. GP, CPN support, day-care, out-patient treatment. Cond disch., fine.	Hostel, hospital, residential home. In/out patient treatment, GP, CPN support, day-care. Abs/cond discharge.
	LOW	MEDIUM	HIGH
	Seriousness of condition		

Figure 6.1 Possible outcomes

(both open and locked) to the much more intrusive provision of the Regional Secure Units and Special Hospitals. This is not to deny the invaluable support networks provided by families, friends and neighbours that enable people to live successfully in the community.

Criminal justice disposals: according to HOC 66/90

> . . . wherever possible, mentally disordered persons should receive care and treatment from the health and social services . . .
> It is recommended that the courts should be encouraged to use the existing provisions of the Mental Health Act, wherever practicable, to enable appropriate mentally disordered persons to be taken into the health system rather than the penal system, and that information should be made available to the courts about the provision of places in special hospitals, regional secure units and local hospitals. (Home Office Circular 66/90. Provision for Mentally Disordered Offenders. 3 September 1990.)

Notwithstanding this, mentally disordered offenders do appear in Court and are dealt with by means of criminal justice, rather than Mental Health Act disposals. Since the advent of the Criminal Justice Act 1991, the seriousness of a defendant's offending should determine the broad band of the sentence (i.e. fines/discharges; community sentences [probation orders, probation orders with additional conditions, supervision orders, community service orders, combination orders]; custody) with factors such as a defendant's mental health condition then being taken into account to mitigate the extent of that seriousness. The point of this is that a defendant's mental health problems should not increase the likelihood of Courts resorting to the use of custodial sentencing. In the past, not knowing what else to do has often been used to excuse a harsher penalty than the offence warranted. Unfortunately, despite a changed sentencing structure and the enjoinders of the Home Office cited above, this has not altogether disappeared.

Similarly, when it comes to a question of bail it has been spelled out time and time again:

> Mentally disordered persons have the same rights as other persons, including a right to bail. A mentally disordered person should never be remanded to prison simply to receive medical treatment or assessment. (Home Office Circular 66/90. Provision for Mentally Disordered Offenders, para 7.)

Clearly, in order to respond to this wide range of need and provision, what is required is a good multi-faceted assessment procedure. Whether this is all the responsibility of one person or the co-ordinated efforts of a number of specialists will depend on local circumstances and resources (there are brief descriptions of different approaches to this aspect of the work elsewhere in this book). An aspect of this comprehensive, multi-faceted assessment that has not been mentioned yet, and that raises once again the warning in the words of Jean Collins quoted earlier, is the cultural or racial aspect. Equal opportunities and anti-discriminatory practice are high on the agenda of most, if not all, of the agencies involved in this work and should recognise that this demands more than just ensuring that whatever is available is on offer to everyone equally, important though that is too. Beyond this, what is important is that someone's cultural or racial sense of identity is not dismissed, compromised or undermined either by the approach to diagnostic assessment (for example, there are a number of studies showing that black people are more likely to be labelled 'mentally ill' than white people and white people are more likely to be labelled psychopath than black people) or by the facilities employed as a response.

Whose responsibility

The principal responsibilities to be considered in this section are assessment and provision but this will also be followed by some thoughts about the gaps that this current structure leaves and who else steps in.

Assessment

Responsibilities for assessment can come either from legislation or local practice guidelines/agreements. Under the National Health Service and Community Care Act 1990 (S47) the responsibility for assessment of community care needs rests explicitly with the local authority. This responsibility has a second element to it:

> having regard to the results of that assessment, shall then decide whether his needs call for the provision by them of any such services. (National Health Service and Community Care Act 1990: Section 47 1(b))

The Police and Criminal Evidence Act requires a Custody Officer to call for an FME immediately if a detained person appears to be suffering from a mental disorder. If it is an urgent case then that detained person must be sent to hospital. The Mental Health Act 1983 gives assessment responsibilities to Approved Social Workers and doctors approved under Section 12. FMEs do not have to be so approved, although some are.

These responsibilities for assessment direct effort principally at the individual person. Notwithstanding the provision of S47 of the NHS and Community Care Act quoted above, this does not necessarily mean that there always will be compatible provision available.

Clearly, assessment is only of any use if it can be used to inform and influence decisions; such decisions are not always to be made by those undertaking the assessments. Consequently good communication systems between assessors and decision-makers need to be established. There already exist some facilities for this, such as Bail Information Schemes, and some assessments are requested by decision-makers.

Provision

Under S46 of the NHS and Community Care Act 1990 each local authority is required to publish a 'plan for the provision of community care services in their area', and they should do this in consultation with the district health authority, family health services authority, local housing authority and interested local voluntary agencies. In this context, 'community care services' means:

Services which a local authority may provide or arrange to be provided under any of the following provisions:

(a) Part III of the National Assistance Act 1948
(b) Section 45 of the Health Services and Public Health Act 1968
(c) Section 21 of, and Schedule 8 to, the National Health Service Act 1977
(d) Section 117 of the Mental Health Act 1983.
(NHS and Community Care Act 1990: S46 (3))

Clearly the important parts here are (a) which includes the provision of accommodation and welfare services for mentally disordered persons, and (d) after-care following detention in hospital. This published plan is of importance because it describes the scope within which the second part of the S47 assessment takes place (the decision about providing a response to the identified need). Anyone involved in a diversion from custody project would do well to read a copy of the published plan for their local area. (It would also be helpful to have sight of the Area Accommodation Strategy which should have been produced following the instruction in Home Office Circular 35/1988 to Probation Committees to establish a local forum for offender accommodation in consultation with other interested parties.)

The search for this kind of combination of facilities will not be necessary, of course, if the appropriate provision is deemed to be admission to hospital: it will, however, at the point of discharge.

The gaps

Perhaps the principal gap in this comes when someone with difficulties does not have the 'needs' that can be responded to with the available provision. Those who are least likely to be provided for in these circumstances are people with challenging behaviour in need of a long term supportive environment. There is provision for people whose condition is seen as treatable, who are likely to get better, but very little for those whose condition is destined not to change or to change very slowly.

Who else steps in?

There are voluntary agencies who provide hostel accommodation, from the general emergency facilities of the Salvation Army and Church Army to the more specifically orientated provision of such organisations as MIND and MENCAP. There is also the supported environment provided by the Richmond Fellowship. Alongside these are the many private residential nursing homes seeking to offer very specific types of facilities.

The extent to which any of these are likely to be able to persist with the difficult behaviour displayed by the many clients of a diversion from custody project will vary according to a whole host of factors, including their resources, why they think they are in business and the abilities of their staff. A consequence of this can be that some people end up doing the round of all the options hoping to find one that can accommodate them long enough for them to settle down.

What can be done with inadequate provision?

The question of inadequate provision or resources is of relevance both in respect of the resources that any Diversion from Custody project may have and of the facilities available to be accessed by mentally disordered offenders. Each is important because it is likely to affect what can be taken into account by the police, Crown Prosecution Service and the Courts, who actually make the decisions about diversion.

Some areas will seek to enhance their response to mentally disordered offenders without employing any additional resources. Regrettable though this may be, in some instances it may just be a realistic appreciation of the situation. The client group will still be there and it is just as important for them not to be disadvantaged. At the very least it is important that someone has the responsibility (a multi-agency steering group does not, itself, demand extra resources) for co-ordinating the information and services that are available and ensuring that they are used to best effect for mentally disordered offenders. This may have to include some changes to local working practices in some agencies so it is important that a steering group has a real collective commitment to the aims of this work even if the agencies cannot invest additional resources.

The co-ordination of information not only requires pooling it, as is proposed in HOC 66/90:

> Information about facilities for accommodation, treatment, education, supervision, etc. should be pooled, and there should be a shared list of contact points with telephone numbers for each agency. (Home Office Circular 66/1990: Provision for Mentally Disordered Offenders. para 17.)

It also requires channelling it to the right places to influence decisions. In the absence of additional resources to establish any new procedure it is vital that existing systems and structures are well understood, fit together well and made use of expressly to enhance the likelihood of diversion work. In this context such systems and procedures as referrals to Psychiatrists and CPNs, accessing community care assessments and bail information schemes are all critical.

Most people involved in this work will think that there is a paucity of appropriate accommodation available in their area for mentally disordered offenders. Irrespective of the scale of the diversion project, the first task is to conduct an audit of what is available and to share the information that comes from it. However bad the situation is, it can only be made better by knowing about all the facilities that can legitimately be accessed by mentally disordered offenders. Beyond this there are efforts that can be made in order to improve the situation. The weight of the agencies represented on the steering group can be used to lobby accommodation providers such as housing authorities and associations with a view to improving access to their facilities. Having these organisations represented on the steering group can help in this. That influence could also be used to lobby the local forum for offender accommodation so that the area accommodation strategy explicitly addresses the needs of mentally disordered offenders.

Treatment and support services in all areas are the victims of restricted budgets and mentally disordered offenders tend not be a popular client group. Even so there are steps that can be taken to make the best of whatever situation exists. Representatives of each agency could ensure that the resources over which they have influence are used to address the needs of mentally disordered offenders. These are likely to be key people from the purchasing authority as well as providers such as Consultant Psychiatrists, Managers of CPN services and SSD Resource Managers. Such access to these people will bring an improved understanding of the priorities and criteria used in their decision-making so that referrals to their provision stand the best chance of success. It is also important to use the weight of the senior management representing the important local agencies on the steering group to lobby the provider agencies in the interests of mentally disordered offenders.

Community Care assessments are meant to be the route for accessing not only comprehensive assessment of a person's needs but also the appropriate provision to respond to those needs. The willingness and ability to pay for those facilities will inevitably be constrained by budgetary considerations. Len Cheston (1993) draws attention to the situation in London where the only way to get one particular authority to pay for drug or alcohol residential services is to challenge their decision through judicial review. Bureaucratic though this may be, it is important that members of such a multiple-disadvantaged client-group are given every chance to benefit from the facilities that do exist.

Conclusion

This chapter has sought to establish that it is important to be bothered about the question — diversion into what? — both in terms of the effectiveness of a project and the appropriate response to individual circumstances. In order to cater for the wide range of individual circumstances there needs to be a broad spectrum of provision available and good multi-faceted assessment to access that provision. Local authorities have the responsibility under the NHS and Community Care Act to provide the assessment that forms the main plank of identifying need and matching provision to it. As hospital is likely to be applicable for a minority of clients of a diversion project the operation of this assessment procedure is both crucial and needed urgently. Ultimately what is needed is an integrated approach that takes a long-term view of an individual's situation. A series of stop-gaps may be good enough to get over the crises but is not really adequate with life being a long-term venture.

At a local level it has to be worth making the effort to do something even if there is no immediate prospect of additional resources with which to do it. At the very least it is important to make sure that the best possible use is made of what there is through co-ordinated effort. The current fragmented service is bound to lead to people missing out unnecessarily; not being able to profit from the facilities that do exist.

7 Funding and managing a project

Funding

Introduction

Issues relating to funding are always fraught with difficulty. No social welfare or criminal justice agency ever considers itself to be adequately funded. Funding is a political as well as a financial problem.

From time to time additional money may be available to fund service developments which meet a need which is high on the political agenda. This additional funding may be on a very large and permanent scale, for example prison building, or on a very small and temporary basis, such as one year 'pump-priming' money to cover part of the costs of a diversion scheme. Short-term funding often materialises following a public or media outcry that 'something must be done' about a current social issue. This can be a problem unless continuing funding can be found.

Instead of developing coherent strategies to measure the problem and giving serious thought to how best to provide a long-term solution, government departments tend to be instructed to respond with speedy one-off grants which concentrate on the particular problem sometimes as if it existed in isolation. This is a situation which can work to the advantage of a steering group who have a flexible development plan. Short-term funding can be useful in the early stages of the development of a diversion system. It should, however, always be viewed as a brief stage of development, not the answer to the problem of funding.

The ultimate ambition of a steering group should be an independent budget, managed with multi-agency agreement and covering all the staff and support costs of a diversion system.

Developing a system within existing resources

The suggested model of development of a diversion from custody system in Chapter 2, relies largely on the effective use of existing staff resources. This is attractive for two reasons, senior management in the relevant agencies are more likely to be willing to work co-operatively with each other to develop a coherent approach to diverting mentally disordered offenders from custody, if they feel they are not going to be asked to find additional funding from within over-stretched budgets.

If a project is to become a system of diversion it must become an integral part of the practice of each agency. In order for it to be worthwhile for all agencies to alter their existing practice to integrate with a system of diversion, the system must have a long-term future.

Developing a diversion project with existing staff resources will be a challenge to effective management in each agency but it is likely to be more useful in the long-run than seeking external short-term funding. However, care should be taken to avoid a situation where fully stretched professionals are expected to provide a specialist service for mentally disordered offenders in addition to their own routine case-load.

Using existing staff to establish a diversion system will only work if they are given clear job descriptions and a manageable work-load.

Short-term funding

Short-term funding, for one to three years is available from a number of sources. These include the Department of Health and major charities such as the Mental Health Foundation. The Home Office also provides some funding which is not currently time-limited.

Short-term funding is usually directed towards very specific functions, for example, to pay a psychiatrist to attend Court. If the purpose for which the funding is available fits into the diversion system which a multi-agency group has designed, it is well worth the effort of applying for it.

However, there is little point in applying for specific funding in the hope of using it for something else. If the intention to use it for some purpose not specified by the funders is apparent from the application, the bid will fail. If the misuse of funding is discovered after a bid has been successful the money will have to be repaid.

Therefore, it is important to be sure when applying for short-term funding that the specific purpose will contribute to a coherent strategy for diversion and that your steering group can actually use the money within the term of the grant.

The chances of success when applying for funding will be increased if it is clear on the application that the bid has the support of a broadly based multi-agency steering group, even if one agency makes the bid on behalf of all the others.

A clear, concise, detailed application has more chance of success than one which is muddled, lengthy and unspecific.

There are some advantages in short-term funding. Senior management may be more ready to help develop a project if funding for one or two extra staff is available, at least initially. If short-term external funding is obtained by the steering group it may give doubters in some agencies the confidence to experiment with change. The knowledge that the grant-making committee of a trust or senior administrators in the Department of Health or Home Office have found an application for short-term funding attractive, may help to strengthen the case of the steering group when arguing the merits of the project. A period of short-term funding for extra staff may give the steering group an opportunity to prove the effectiveness of the project they are proposing.

However, short-term funding may be a trap for the unwary. Firstly, it may encourage some local agencies to feel that someone else is taking care of the problem. Secondly, it is merely postponing the inevitable battle to obtain local funding, not settling the issue permanently.

Long-term funding

The ideal pattern of funding for a diversion system is for it to be funded adequately and securely. There are several ways of achieving this.

Secondment of staff

If a multi-agency team, such as that in the North Humberside Project is formed, it may be possible for each agency to second an existing member of staff to the team. If that person later wishes to move on, the seconding agency will replace that person, enabling the team to be kept up to strength.

There will be some issues to be resolved before agreement can be reached on secondment.

If one agency is to act as host to the multi-agency team, will there be any additional costs to the host agency? This issue should be discussed and resolved satisfactorily as soon as possible, otherwise it may cause problems which undermine the whole project.

Creation of a 'Diversion Agency'

The process of creating a system which achieves diversion from custody can be achieved incrementally, by an evolutionary process which enables each stage of development to be built on the success of previous experiments. For example, short-term funding creates a new specialist post, the work undertaken highlights the need for continued funding. Funding for that post is then provided on a more permanent basis by the relevant agency, or a person is seconded to fill the post, under a secondment agreement. More staff from other agencies are then seconded to provide a complete multi-agency team. Thus the use of each type of funding can be a useful tool in the development of the diversion system. The size and composition of the eventual team will depend on the nature and needs of the area it serves.

Agreement about the way in which the project or system is managed will be closely linked to the way in which it is funded. Funding remains the key issue to be settled satisfactorily before a diversion system can develop to fulfil all the needs of an area.

It can appear almost inevitable that the agencies which provide the most funding for a project or system will expect to exert the greatest management control over the project. However, if one agency appears to be too dominant, other agencies may be alienated and their commitment undermined. The delicate balance between funding and management in any multi-agency project is crucial to its success.

One way of distancing the management of a diversion system from the sources of funding is to create a separate mini-agency with its own budget and management structure which is answerable to a steering group drawn from the most senior levels of the relevant agencies.

Whether or not this is a cost-effective approach will depend on the needs of the area and the number of cases.

It may be possible to combine several different types of diversionary work in one mini-agency. This may help to overcome problems with economies of scale and enable a team with a wide range of professional skills to be established.

The Northamptonshire model of combining responsibility in one diversion unit for the diversion of young offenders, with that of mentally disordered offenders, as well as administering a public interest case assessment scheme and a reparation scheme provides an interesting example of a holistic approach to diversion from the criminal justice system.

The Northamptonshire approach is radical and still very new. It remains to be seen whether the interests of mentally disordered offenders are best served by professionals who are part of a generic diversion service or by a specialist team concentrating solely on mental health issues. One of the greatest attractions of the Northamptonshire model is that is contains a balance of autonomy with multi-agency management. It also provides more secure funding and a coherent management structure which overcomes many of the problems of multi-agency management by allowing managers from one profession to manage staff from another profession. It also overcomes a perennial problem of multi-agency funding by giving responsibility for managing a budget contributed to by several agencies to a manager answerable to a steering group representing those agencies but with sufficient managerial autonomy to manage that budget to provide the best possible service.

Management

Introduction

The way in which diversion project staff are managed will have a significant impact on the success and effectiveness of the project.

If it is agreed to apply for additional funding or divert existing funding, to employ, place or second staff to a specialist project, thought must be given at the earliest possible stage as to how these staff should be managed.

It is important that the sense of co-ownership and joint responsibility, which will have been engendered by the joint endeavours of the steering group up to the point of acquiring staff dedicated to a specialist project, is maintained by agreements about how it is to be managed.

A well thought-out management plan will also help to attract and retain good quality staff to the project team.

Direction of the project — the steering group

Overall responsibility for the direction in which the project develops should remain with the steering group. Many of the problems which will arise in the first few months of the development will be within the power of the steering group members, as individuals or as a whole, to solve. It is important, therefore, that they retain their sense of ownership and do not feel that their usefulness as a group has ceased with the successful outcome of an application for funding. Decisions will also have to be taken about different types of boundaries for the project. For example, will it cover one or more Magistrates Court areas? Will it accept referrals relating to mentally disordered offenders aged between sixteen and sixty, or eighteen and sixty-five?

Once these initial decisions have been made and the project has its basic shape, the steering group should turn its attention to how the project should operate.

At this point it may be useful for the steering group to create a sub-committee or management team to which it can delegate many of these decisions. By involving a broadly-based group of representatives from relevant agencies in the management of the project, the co-ownership and joint responsibility will be maintained.

If management responsibility is delegated by the steering group to one manager in one agency, there is a risk that the sense of co-ownership will disappear. There is also a risk that the other agencies will feel that the agency assuming the key management role has assumed complete responsibility for solving all the problems relating to mentally disordered offenders in the criminal justice system.

It would therefore appear wise to continue to develop the Project on as broad a multi-agency base as is practicable and one way of doing this is for the steering group to appoint a sub-committee to take management responsibility for the project as it develops.

If a sub-committee approach is favoured it will be up to the steering group as a whole to decide where it wishes to draw the line between decisions which should be taken by the entire steering group and those which can be more effectively made by a smaller group meeting more frequently.

Once that line has been drawn, arrangements must be agreed for reporting those decisions and subsequent actions to the steering group, so that they continue to be involved and informed.

Detailed development — management team

The management team should ideally be small enough to be able to meet fairly frequently and to get together quickly if necessary. If the project has a CPN, an ASW or a Probation Officer, the management team should contain managers who are qualified to provide professional supervision to each of those staff.

Major stakeholders in the success of the project, such as the Police or Court Clerks, may also have a useful role to play as members of the management team. They will be able to make the necessary arrangements, for example, for access to police stations or the use of a phone at Court.

When the membership of the management team has been agreed by the steering group, the management team must appoint their own chair and agree who will take responsibility for agendas and minutes for their meetings. Although this may seem unnecessarily bureaucratic it will help to keep all the members of the management team fully informed all the time. Such minutes could also be copied to the steering group members for information. If disagreements later arise about who undertook to do what with whom, a full set of clear, concise, cabinet-style minutes will help to keep everyone's memories fresh and minds focused on the necessary actions to be taken.

Although it may be attractive to allow one enthusiast to take responsibility for all the resulting additional work, it will be better in the long term if responsibilities are shared equally. It is always dangerous to rely too much on the input of one person in case that person has to move on. Therefore, the more equitably the work can be distributed, the more effectively the management team will operate in the longer term.

Practical management arrangements

Job description

(See Appendix IV)

The first task of the management team is to draft a job description. This needs to be sufficiently clear to enable anyone who applies for the post to know what is required of them, and sufficiently flexible to allow the project to grow and develop.

It should include the duties of the post and how the post will be managed.

Personnel specification

Before filling the new post or posts it is important to devise a specification of the sort of person who will be suitable for the post. This should be done in such a way that it does not contravene the equal opportunities policies of any of the agencies represented. However, the management team should give serious thought to the combinations of qualities and qualifications which enable the post holder to meet the challenge of working as part of a multi-agency team, or in an unfamiliar environment.

Selection

The management team should make up the selection panel, whether the post-holder is to be placed or seconded with the project by one agency, or employed by the project in its own right.

It may be helpful to divide the selection process into two parts, a short presentation and a formal interview. The presentation may serve two purposes. Firstly, the topic chosen should enable the candidate to display his or her knowledge of the problems of mentally disordered offenders in the criminal justice system. Secondly the presentation will give the management team an opportunity to assess the ability of the candidate to express him or herself coherently and to make a convincing case.

Day-to-day management — the project staff

Arrangements should be made to ensure that the project staff member or members know whom to ask about what. The management team should decide how responsibility for providing day management is to be divided. It may be if the project base is to be in the offices of, for example, Probation, that the probation service member of the management team takes responsibility for arranging administrative support, providing desks and so on. One member of the management team should always be available to all the project staff for advice and support if unforseen problems arise or difficult decisions need to be made.

The project staff will need to have sufficient experience and confidence to be able to operate successfully in a new project which does not follow the usual pattern of line management. They will also need to be self-motivated and to be able to exercise their own judgement without constant referral to their managers. During the early stages of the project, extra support and guidance may be useful, especially if the project involves staff previously unknown to each other, working together co-operatively.

Agreement by the management team of how each project member is expected to function within the project, should be reached at the earliest opportunity, preferably as soon as funding is agreed. This will enable staff to be given the clearest possible remit in a situation where some uncertainty is inevitable.

The Project Team members should meet together regularly to discuss all the issues which affect them. Minutes of their meetings should be kept and circulated to the members of the management team before their meetings. Regular combined meetings involving the project team and the management team should be held, especially in the early months of the project's operation.

Conclusion

Multi-agency management requires considerable ability to communicate and co-operate on the part of the members of the management team in order to be successful and effective. This is not likely to be achieved without some cost to each of the management team members.

There will always be a tension between allegiance to a multi-agency project in which they may have significant personal investment and allegiance to their own individual agency. At the outset each member of the management team must be clear how they intend to cope with that tension.

Individuals who become members of the management team may find themselves in the role of a buffer between their own agency and the project. They may find themselves arguing on behalf of the project with colleagues who are not convinced of its benefits. They may find themselves to be identified so closely with the project that its success or failure will be seen as an indicator of their professional competence.

While this may well be beneficial to a project, the cost to the individual of this role as 'product champion' must not be underestimated.

Members of the management team may not be well known to each other when the team is formed, but they will have to develop a good working relationship quickly if they hope to provide effective leadership for the project. They will have to get used to listening to each other. They will have to get used to not always being right. They will have to get used to making concessions in order to ensure the success of the project. Multi-agency management is a game for grown-ups.

The benefits of multi-agency management should outweigh the costs. The importance of the maintenance of broadly-based support for the project cannot be overstated. Also it will serve as a good example to a project team if they see their managers combining their efforts in the interests of the project, rather than for the benefit of their individual agency.

By working together in this way the management team will be sending clear consistent messages about multi-agency co-operation to the team and to the steering group.

8 Record keeping, monitoring and evaluation

Project Records

Introduction

The diversion project will need a good system of record keeping. The style and method of record keeping, as well as where records will be kept and who will be responsible for maintaining them, should be agreed by the steering group or management team, as appropriate, as early in the life of the project as possible.

A choice will have to be made between using paper records and establishing a data base. The idea of the data base is likely to be very attractive to several of the agencies represented on the steering group. Information about mentally disordered offenders is not usually collected and stored jointly, rather each agency will have only part of the information relating to those mentally disordered offenders who are known to criminal justice, health and social welfare agencies.

However, although the establishment of a data base which would amalgamate all the information available to all the agencies and thereby create a coherent picture of the number of mentally disordered offenders in each locality and the nature of their individual problems is attractive, there are several serious drawbacks to such an approach.

First, clear agreements would have to be reached between the agencies about what information would be stored on the data base and with whom it should be shared. Registration of the data base under the Data Protection Act requires clarity on these matters.

Secondly, the question must be asked, 'what purpose will be served by having a data base which would not be served by keeping paper client records? Will a data base save time or help the diversion staff to work more effectively? Will the establishment of a data base help to provide a more efficient service to clients of the project?' Thirdly, who will be responsible for maintaining the data base, inputting and retrieving information, arranging a back-up and so on? If it is to be the diversion staff, do they have the skills? If not, can they be trained? Who will pay for such training, and for the necessary hardware and software, to establish a data base?

One of the advantages of a data base is that it enables the diversion staff to have access to all the stored knowledge of the other staff about each client.

However, the information must be stored in a way which is easily accessible to diversion staff when they need it. Laptop computers are the only way in which the team can have access to the information they require in the police station, courts and prisons.

The data base is likely to be expensive if it is to be useful. If funding is available for the establishment of a data base it may well be worth pursuing.

If the steering group decide they wish to develop a diversion data base they should draft a very clear remit before seeking professional advice. They should also be clear, before employing anyone to design and establish a data base, who are the parties to the contract, what the finished product should look like and within what timescale it should be delivered.

Any price agreed for the purchase of hardware or software should include any necessary training for all staff required to use the data base and some sort of back-up system to protect the data base in the event of a failure of a hard disk or other catastrophe.

Records of the project

Client case notes, whether stored in files or on a data base should contain as much of the following information as is relevant to each individual.

a) Personal details
   Name, address, date of birth, marital status, gender, ethnic origin, next of kin.
b) Agencies involved
   Solicitor, social services key-worker, GP, psychiatrist, probation officer, key nurse, prison medical officer, others.
c) Psychiatric history
   Known to psychiatric service, diagnosis, risk assessment, voluntary or compulsory patient.

d) Previous convictions, seriousness, pattern of offending, other outstanding charges.
e) Current problems
Accommodation, mental health/learning disability, family, finance, offending, drugs, alcohol, other.
f) Project involvement
Referral, by whom, when made, accepted, case allocated, action taken, outcomes.
g) Police station
Details of arrest, detention, Appropriate Adult, ASW, solicitor, interview, charge, bail, MHA 1983, other outcomes.
h) Magistrates Court
Assessed by Psychiatrist, psychiatric report, report to CPS re: discontinuance plea, bail, conditions remand in custody, which prison, pre-sentence report, MHA 1983, other outcomes.
i) Crown Court
Committed for trial, psychiatric report, bail, remand in custody, sentence, MHA 1983, other outcomes.
j) Prison
Sentence, which prison, liaison with prison medical staff, assessment, transfer, contact with C3, Home Office.

Confidentiality

Because the records of the project will be made up of information from various sources, strict rules about disclosure need to be agreed and adhered to at the outset of the project.

Information about clients of the project should always be treated as confidential and only shared with third parties in limited circumstances, agreed by the steering group, and with the consent of the client of the project.

Disclosure of information

Information held by the project should be confidential unless it is necessary to share information in the interests of the client, for example:

a) To the police, in order to achieve no further action, a caution, or police bail.
b) To the CPS to facilitate public interest case assessment, or support an argument in favour of discontinuance of the prosecution.
c) To the Magistrates Court in the form of written or oral evidence to achieve a non-custodial remand or sentence, including pre-sentence reports.

d) To the prison medical officer in order to obtain appropriate care and support for a mentally disordered offender in custody.
e) Other agencies, e.g. probation, social services and housing providers in order to obtain an adequate package of care for the mentally disordered offender, at any stage in the criminal justice process.

Disclosure of information in these circumstance may be as the result of a legal compulsion, or of a professional responsibility. However, it is good practice to obtain the consent to the disclosure of the client of the project whenever possible.

Consent to disclosure

The issue of consent to the disclosure of information is linked to the broader issue of consent to involvement by the project in the life of the client of the project. In order to give consent a mentally disordered offender must have the legal capacity to give his or her consent whether to disclosure in particular or intervention on his or her behalf in general. A person is presumed to be generally capable of making decisions for him/herself unless proved otherwise. Tests of capacity can be made by people who are not mental health professionals.

A legal incapacity arises whenever the law provides that a person is incapable of taking a particular decision, undertaking a particular act or engaging in a particular activity. Capacity is relative to the person, the decision and the time. Capacity must be judged in relation to the particular activity or decision involved.

The law adopts a 'functional' rather than a 'status' test. The ability to process information and make choices in a self-controlled or autonomous way is crucial, not the person's 'status', e.g. a prisoner, or detained under the MHA 1983.

There should always be a presumption that consent must be obtained from the client before the project can intervene on his/her behalf, except where there is a statutory duty to act and the client's consent is not required. Clients should be informed of the statutory duty to act, and about the action taken, even though there is no obligation to obtain the client's consent.

Consent must be obtained before information about the client is shared with other persons or agencies outside the project, staff team/management group, except where there is a statutory or agency-imposed duty to disclose that information. Where such a duty exists the client should be informed of it even though his/ her consent is not required to the disclosure.

In order to have full capacity to consent, a client should be able to understand:

1. That they are in the criminal justice system, and why, and the consequences which may result.
2. What alternatives are being offered and be able to express preferences, make choices or reach agreements.
3. The consequences of not consenting to intervention by the project on his/her behalf.
4. The consequences of not doing what s/he has agreed to do.

Incapacity

Capacity may vary in a person from day-to-day. When a client's incapacity appears to be continuous, decisions will then have to be taken by the project staff/management group about who else should be involved, e.g. social service re: guardianship, and what intervention may properly be made without consent. Continuous and profound incapacity may suggest that a client is unfit to plead (Insanity and Unfitness to Plead Act 1991).

Monitoring

In order for the evaluation to be as useful and effective as possible, joint records should be kept up-to-date and accurately in an agreed format.

The standard of record keeping and the adequacy of the information contained in clients' case notes should be monitored on a regular basis by the steering group or management team as appropriate.

If interim reports are required by the steering group or by funders of the project, the records should be able to answer all the necessary questions. These will include:

1. How many referrals have been made to the project, by whom and when?
2. How many have been diverted
   (a) from the police station?
   (b) from the Magistrates Court?
   (c) from prison?
3. Outcomes and reasons — e.g. bailed, hospital orders, remands in custody etc?
4. Re-offending — how many clients have re-offended, nature and frequency of offence?

The answers to these questions will inform the local debate about the value and effectiveness of the project. However, the answers will not always be simple. A mentally disordered offender may be remanded in custody briefly until seen by a psychiatrist, or until appropriate housing or social care may be arranged. Although such a remand in custody may be regarded as a sort of failure, it needs to be viewed in context. In the absence of a 'control group' of clients for whom no diversionary intervention is made, it will be impossible for monitoring of the project to measure accurately the numbers of people diverted by the project or system who would otherwise have been remanded or sentenced to custody. It is important, therefore, to have an independent evaluation which can review the activity of the project and measure its success in broader terms then mere numbers.

The steering group and the project need to be realistic about what can be arranged and achieved and within what timescales. The Courts are likely to err on the side of caution. This picture may change as the project becomes more established and other agencies become more confident in the ability of the project to deliver. The issue of risk cannot be avoided, but it cannot be settled objectively. There are always going to be professional differences of opinion about the degree of risk to self or others presented by a mentally disordered offender. Such differences may make a difference to the outcome for the mentally disordered offender but a failure to divert may not reflect badly on the effectiveness of the project staff.

It may well be that the risk was considered too great by the Court, or that no suitable alternative to custody was available.

The diversion project staff should avoid making recommendations to the Court which are clearly not going to be accepted, bearing in mind the mental health and offending matrix. If the recommendations of the project are viewed as balanced and realistic, the confidence of the Courts is likely to increase. There are often no simple answers to the problems of mentally disordered offenders. Their offending may be the product of a lifetime of unresolved problems. It is over-ambitious of any project to set out to provide all the answers immediately for such individuals.

Successful diversion for some may not be achieved until the third of fourth attempt. The mentally disordered offender may decide to stop taking his or her medication at some time in the future in which case his or her condition may deteriorate and problems may mount up again, culminating in re-offending. This is the particular challenge of the client group. There will be gratifying successes, there will also be disheartening failure. What should be remembered at all times is that the efforts of each agency acting singly, have never managed to address the complex problems of mentally disordered offenders. By combining the skills and talents of different disciplines and by establishing effective communications and a sense of shared responsibility, the diversion project or system will provide a quantum leap in terms of the effectiveness of the service to the client. Therefore although the project may not be completely effective, it is almost certainly going to be able to achieve better outcomes than those which have been achieved before. This is not an argument for complacency, but it should be borne in mind when judging the effectiveness of a diversion system or project.

Evaluation

Introduction

Thorough evaluation is essential to the continued success of the diversion project once it has been established. Unfortunately evaluation is often used as a weapon rather than a tool, so the word evaluation becomes a threat rather than a promise.

Any new approach to an old problem is likely to meet with opposition and inertia from the majority of people working in criminal justice, health and social welfare agencies. This may be partly because a new approach is seen as a condemnation of old methods, partly because some of the more put-upon agencies will fear that they are going to be asked to do more and partly because of the general fear that fashionable specialities drain resources from those doing the real work.

Evaluation from the outset is crucial to overcoming resistance and suspicion at all levels. All the agencies concerned will have to have a measurable perceivable benefit from all the effort involved in setting up a system, changing working practices and finding funding for additional staff. Evaluation needs to be written in to all the plans at the earliest stage.

Remit of the evaluation

A non-specific evaluation will be an expensive waste of time. It is important for the steering group to agree a clear and simple remit for the evaluation.

It has been suggested that the aims and objectives of any diversion system should be to divert mentally disordered offenders from prosecution, inappropriate remand and sentences to custody, and to help prevent re-offending.

The first question for any evaluation is 'have these aims and objectives been achieved?' The second question is,'if not, why not?' and the third and last question is 'what else needs to be done to enable the answer to the first question to be broadly "yes"?' The answers to the first question will lie in the records of the project (see records p. 83). For example the records will show the numbers of prosecutions discontinued following intervention or representations from the diversion staff.

The answers to the second question will also largely appear in those same records. For example, the records will show how many mentally disordered offenders were assessed and diagnosed as suitable for admission to hospital under the MHA 1983, and considered to require a secure bed but none were available.

Even when the answers to questions are qualitative rather than quantitive, for example, unhelpful attitudes of the police, or the unwillingness of housing providers to take risks, the records of the project if properly kept will reflect these problems as well as those relating to lack of appropriate provision. The problems with access to services for mentally disordered offenders which militate against diversion are as often to do with attitudes of service providers as they are to do with the availability of service provision.

Choosing an evaluator

Once having drafted a remit for the evaluation, the steering group will have to choose who is to undertake the evaluation.

The quality of the evaluation may depend to some extent on how much money is available to spend on it, but there is no absolute correlation between price and quality. All agencies will have access to the names of professional evaluators. Otherwise advice can be sought from the Mental Health Foundation, Good Practices in Mental Health or the Kings Fund College (see useful addresses in Appendix V).

Suggested criteria for evaluator

1. Good working knowledge of criminal justice, health and social welfare systems.
2. Understanding of relevant legislation.
3. Ability to communicate effectively with people at all levels in the relevant agencies and with mentally disordered offenders.
4. Ability to write clearly and concisely.
5. Presentation skills.
6. Experience in establishing or operating paper record-keeping systems and data bases.
7. Experience in carrying out evaluation.
   It is very important to find out what work an evaluator has carried out in the past and to find out from those who have commissioned other evaluations, how well those pieces of work have been done.

Commissioning the evaluation

When the evaluator has been chosen and the remit of the evaluation agreed, the steering group, or whoever is officially commissioning the evaluation must draw up the terms of their agreement with the evaluator.

This agreement should include the names of the evaluators, the agreed price and date of completion of the evaluation. The remit should be very clear and specific and should be included as part of the agreement.

It is not usually wise to pay for an evaluation before it is completed satisfactorily.

There are several reasons for identifying and engaging an evaluator at the beginning of the project. It is useful to be able to assure funders and other doubters that an independent evaluation is to be carried out. Also it can help to concentrate the minds of all those involved on working together effectively. No one agency or person will wish to be identified as a cause of problems with or even failure of a diversion project or system.

On a more positive note the evaluator may be able to give constructive assistance with the establishing of record keeping systems. This will be of benefit to the project but it will also greatly assist the evaluator who will be able to ensure that the information recorded is the information necessary to complete the evaluation within the terms of the remit specified by the steering group.

The evaluator will need to know about everyone involved in establishing and operating the diversion system as well as all the other professionals affected by it, for example Custody Officers. The evaluator will have to take samples of attitudes towards issues relating to diversion and mental disorder generally at the time at which the project is being developed. This will give an overall picture of the situation before the project becomes fully operational, in order to provide a measure of the progress made by the project when the views of those same people are taken again at the end of the first year of the project.

The evaluation report

When it is finally delivered, the evaluation should be proof read for accuracy, edited for brevity and summarised for convenience. The two most useful parts of any evaluation are the summary and the statistics. The statistics should be laid out in such a way that they clearly answer the questions asked by the remit.

9 The future of the project

When the evaluation has been completed, the steering group will have more work to do in addressing the issues raised by the evaluation.

If the evaluation demonstrates that the project or system is working very well there will still be underlying problems to be addressed. Some of these problems may be beyond the power of the steering group to solve, for example if the evaluation highlights the need for a psychiatric bail hostel but no funding is available for such a resource.

The evaluation may have proved painful or embarrassing for some agencies or individuals if it highlighted an inadequate service or failure to follow agreed practice guidelines. Those issues will have to be addressed speedily and effectively with the minimum of recriminations. It is important that the steering group maintains a positive united approach to problem solving and does not fall apart because some agencies come out of the evaluation better than others.

The experiences of the first year of the project may be very mixed but they will at least provide a useful basis for further development.

Future development of the project

However successful the system or project which is adopted is in terms of diversion from custody and the prevention of re-offending, the project will need to change and develop over time. It is axiomatic to the establishment of a new project that those problems which are anticipated will not materialise and those problems which no-one could have foreseen will cause enormous amounts of work.

If the multi-agency steering group has been able to cope with all the uncertainty of a new project and produce good results at the end of its first year, it may well be tempted to rest on its laurels. There may be a consensus that everyone has worked hard and done very well and therefore deserves a rest. However, although the frantic activity necessary to establish the project and get it successfully through its early days should not need to be maintained, there will probably be a continued role for the steering group in the future.

In any event, the completion of the first year of the life of the project and the successful completion of the evaluation should be a cause for some sort of celebratory event to which Senior Managers, Magistrates and other opinion formers can be invited. Such a celebration would help to remind the wider world of the existence and success of the project.

The purpose of such a celebration is to look back with pride on the achievements of the project so far. The next step is to look forward and ask the questions 'whither the steering group?, whither the Project?'

The answers to both will depend on the level of development of the project. If the project is running reasonably smoothly, if funding is agreed for more than one year and if the management team are confident in their role there will be very little remaining work which relates directly to the project for the steering group to do.

If, however, the project is still experiencing major problems, or if there are still fundamental decisions to be made about its role or remit following the evaluation, the steering group will have to maintain its commitment and involvement in the project for as long as it is needed.

This may seem a daunting prospect but it need not be. As the steering group becomes more experienced and effective, solving problems and overcoming difficulties should become easier. Also, continued close involvement in the project will help to maintain the commitment and sense of joint responsibility which will have been crucial to the success of the project so far.

If the steering group feels that the project no longer requires close supervision, it has two basic choices. First, it can cease to exist, and secondly it can metamorphose into something else by developing a new role. It can be argued that the first option though it may initially be attractive is not the best one. Even if the project or system is functioning very well, that may not always continue to be the case. Unforseen problems may arise in the future and without its own steering group such a specialist project will always be vulnerable to attack from cost-cutting exercises and internal re-organisation within each agency responsible for funding or providing staff. There may also still be a great deal to be achieved.

If the project was focused on one Magistrates Court area, does another adjacent one require a similar service? Would funding be available for such an expansion? Is some piece of the diversion jigsaw still missing? Would the presence of a psychiatrist at Court be of assistance? If so, would funding be available from health authority or central government sources? Is there a shortage of suitable bail accommodation? If so, could the steering group draft proposals for a specialist bail hostel?

Having asked itself and answered these questions, the steering group may discover that there is still a great deal of practical work for them to do in order to develop and strengthen the project to achieve its potential.

If the outcome of the examination of the future role of the steering group is that the role for which it was established no longer exists, it will have two choices, to cease to exist or to evolve to perform another function.

Although disbanding the steering group at this stage may be an attractive option to those members who are over-committed in other areas of work, there will still be cogent reasons for keeping it going. First, the pattern of multi-agency working and co-operation which will have been established is worth maintaining.

Secondly, the problems of mentally disordered offenders are not going to go away for ever when an effective project or system is in place. The needs of those people will still have to be addressed in a coherent and united way. The issue of mentally disordered offenders is currently generating high levels of interest in the media and among the public. What will happen when that interest has waned, or attention is focused on some other area of social concern. The diversion system or project will need strong advocates in order to maintain the commitment of all the agencies to its continued success.

Thirdly, however effective the project, unforseen problems will arise from time to time. The steering group will be a useful forum for addressing those issues and looking for positive solutions. Relationships within the group should have become sufficiently robust for differences of opinion to be expressed, and settled views challenged within the group without such differences and challenges becoming too destructive.

Multi-agency working can become very comfortable and familiar but it should not be allowed to become too cosy. There still needs to be some creative tension to generate new thoughts and ideas within the group.

There is no point in keeping the steering group going for these theoretical benefits alone. Hard working professionals need to see some practical as well as some theoretical benefits from their work.

The steering group therefore needs to find a new role for itself if it is going to be able to build on all its achievements and maintain the benefits of multi-agency working.

One way forward for the steering group is for it to become a group which formulates policy. In order for this to be able to happen, each agency will have to delegate to each representative a limited authority to negotiate on behalf of each agency, possible changes in policy, procedure and practice which the work of the diversion project or system has highlighted as desirable.

The agreement of joint practices and procedures would be a massive undertaking, involving understanding the complex interrelationships between the agencies and between legal requirements and practical implementation.

However, by developing such a structure of practice and procedures, the steering group would be moving diversion from custody from the realms of *ad hoc* agreements and informal networks to the more secure arena of joint policy development. There will therefore need to be less reliance on individual effort and good will to ensure the effectiveness of the diversion system. An agreed policy and procedures manual, adhered to by every agency, which will protect the rights and safeguard the interests of every mentally disordered offender, would help to ensure a secure future for diversion from custody (see suggested model contents for Practice and Procedure Guide, Appendix VI).

If every agency is prepared to change and modify its practice in order to facilitate diversion, the principles of diversion will become accepted as the norm.

Membership of the forum should be at an appropriate level of seniority. In order to function effectively it will require as much commitment as was required to ensure the successful working of the steering group.

Developing agreed policies and procedures is not likely to be overwhelmingly exciting. However, it will be necessary for all the forum members to apply themselves consistently and diligently to the necessary work.

It may be useful to divide into special interest groups to develop each part of the policy and procedure guide, in order to speed up the process and share the burden of work fairly and evenly.

The pace of such work need not be unduly fast but it should still make discernable progress otherwise members of the forum may lose heart and interest. The role of the Chair will be crucial to the successful development of the forum and to the eventual production of a worthwhile and enduring piece of work.

The model remit for a Forum (see Appendix VII) suggests that the Chair is elected at an AGM and holds office for a year at a time.

During the life of the group, which has developed from working party to steering group and has now become a forum, the skills and attributes required of a Chair will have changed substantially. In the early stages of its development a diversion group needs as its Chair a person who has some standing within the group, who has sufficient authority to bind a disparate group together to form an effective whole.

Such a person could be described as a 'mover and shaker' because of their ability to inspire belief in the idea that change is possible and that something can be done to address the needs of mentally disordered offenders and divert them from custody.

When it has completed its metamorphosis from steering group to forum it may require a Chair with different types of skills. If the forum has adopted the broad principles of diversion from custody, and has grown used to working together, discussing new ideas and developing new solutions, it may not need to have an inspiring or charismatic Chair. The forum may no longer require a leader, it may need a co-worker instead.

The ideal Chair for the forum would be someone who has sufficient status and authority to keep the forum together and maintain the momentum of development of the policy and procedure guides. He or she should also have the staying power to keep everyone working until the goal is achieved. The Chair of the forum should be a 'completer/finisher'.

Throughout this book the value of flexibility and a willingness to work with others co-operatively to overcome apparently insuperable problems has been constantly stressed. It cannot be overemphasised. An agreement on policies or procedures will go a large part of the way to ensuring a better outcome than custody for mentally disordered offenders, but it is co-operation and flexibility which completes the picture of success.

All the agencies involved in the criminal justice, health and social care systems will need to continue to foster this spirit of co-operation and flexibility if the progress made in diversion is to be maintained in the years to come. Diversion from custody for mentally disordered offenders may cease to be a fashionable course. A strong and responsive forum will be vital if the interests of mentally disordered offenders are to be safeguarded in the future. The aim of this book has been to provide a practical guide for those professionals who wish to work together to divert mentally disordered offenders from custody and provide some hope of a better, more constructive model of care. There will never be any easy answers to the complex problems of mentally disordered offenders. However, the development of projects and systems may achieve real change in the way in which people are treated and create hope of a more enlightened system in the future. Such development will need to be informed by new approaches, and develop to meet changing need.

Above all, vigilance is vital if mentally disordered offenders are not to return to the obscurity they have suffered for the past two hundred years — out of sight and out of mind.

Appendix I

CASE STUDY

Andrew — aged 33 — single — NFA

Presenting situation

Andrew is in custody in a police station following arrest for breaking windows and calling out the fire brigade.

Case history and background information

Andrew is a man in his thirties. He has had a criminal record for the past ten years. He has one conviction for arson which leads to a five-year prison sentence. He is very overweight, heavily bearded and is perceived by some as having a frightening, threatening appearance. He often finds it difficult to communicate and withdraws into a state of sullen isolation. He likes being in prison. He is afraid of people and prefers the prison segregation unit where he does not dress and will use any available implement to inflict superficial wounds upon himself. His chest and arms are covered by old and new scars.

On release from prison after each sentence Andrew has actively sought to regain the security of the segregation unit or hospital wing. Apart from the arson his offences have mostly been minor. When angry or frustrated he breaks windows. He has a fascination for the fire brigade. When last released he managed in a private residential home for three weeks before calling out the fire brigade.

Group task

1. How should your agency become involved and what can you do for Andrew?
2. Who else would need to be involved and what would they have to do?
3. What would the aim and objectives of such intervention be?
4. How could all the agencies who need to be involved improve their communication and co-operation to work together to help Andrew?

Appendix II

AREA CRIMINAL JUSTICE LIAISON COMMITTEE

Survey of diversion activity

1.	Name	Agency/address telephone number	Position	Areas covered

2. Steering group

Does a multi-agency steering group on diversion from custody for mentally disordered offenders operate in your area?

Yes ☐ No ☐

3. Geographical area

If yes, please describe the geographical and service area limits of its operation area.

a) Magistrates Court area ☐

b) Probation area ☐

c) Social services area ☐

d) Police division ☐

e) District health authority ☐

f) Health trust (provider) area ☐

g) Other(s) please specify ☐

Tick more than one box if appropriate.

4. Membership — tick all relevant boxes

Organisation	Position of representative (e.g. police rank, job title etc)	
Police	....	☐
CPS	....	☐
Justices Clerks	....	☐
Probation service	....	☐
Social service	....	☐
District health authority	....	☐
Health trust	....	☐
Voluntary organisation	....	☐
Prison	....	☐
Other (e.g. university)	....	☐

5. Remit

Does your steering group have a specific remit?

Yes ☐ No ☐

If yes, please summarise

....

....

....

6. Time scale

How long has it been meeting

Less than six months ☐

Six months – one year ☐

One year – two years ☐

More than two years ☐

7. Current position — diversion from custody

What diversionary arrangements are currently in place.

a) Diversion from police station

(i) CPN visiting police stations ☐

(ii) ASW visiting police stations ☐

(iii) Appropriate Adult arrangements ☐

(Please specify which police stations if possible)

....

....

....

b) Bail and discontinuance

(i) Bail information scheme
[................................] Magistrates Court ☐

(ii) CPN available at Court (hours/days per week)

.... ☐

(iii) Psychiatrist available at [...........................] ☐
Magistrates Court (hours/days per week)

....

(iv) System for communicating information to CPS ☐
— relating to discontinuance
— Public Interest Case Assessment

c) Sentencing Advice

(i) System for providing information to
Magistrates Court for sentencing decisions ☐

(ii) System for providing information to Crown
Court for sentencing decisions ☐

(iii) Specialist probation officer available ☐

d) Alternatives to custody and sentencing in the community

(i) Medium secure hospital beds
How many? ☐ Where?......................... ☐

(ii) Low secure hospital beds
How many? ☐ Where?......................... ☐

(iii) Acute admission beds
How many? ☐ Where?......................... ☐

(iv) Rehabilitation beds
How many? ☐ Where?......................... ☐

(v) Sub acute beds
How many? ☐ Where?......................... ☐

(vi) Bail hostel beds
How many? ☐ Where?......................... ☐

(vii) Other bail accommodation beds
How many? ☐ Where?......................... ☐

(viii) Specialist supported housing beds
How many? ☐ Where?......................... ☐

(ix) Other long term accommodation

(x) Day care places

Probation — how many? ☐

Social services — how many? ☐

Voluntary organisation? ☐

(xi) Community mental health teams
How many? ☐ Where?......................... ☐

(xii) Other services not listed here
How many places? ☐ Where?................. ☐

e) Custody

(i) Prison/remand centre ☐
Name..

(ii) Bail information scheme available? ☐

(iii) Referral arrangements with local
in-patient facility? ☐

(iv) Visiting Psychiatrist? ☐

8. Evaluation

Are any of your diversionary arrangements being monitored and evaluated. By Whom? When? ☐

....

....

....

9. Development

a) Developments planned ☐

Please give brief details, funding obtained and time scales

....

....

....

b) Further information/advice ☐

Do you require information and advice on funding and/or development of systems to divert mentally disordered offenders from custody? ☐

Return to:

Appendix III

Mentally disordered offender — information for Court — CPS and defence

Defendant: ______________________________

Offence: ______________________________

First appearance ☐ Remand ☐ Commital ☐ Other ☐ __________

Court: ______________________________ Date: __________

____

Previous contact with psychiatric services Yes ☐ No ☐

Name/Address Psychiatrists: ______________________________

____

District Health Authority: ______________________________

Symptoms of mental disorder: Yes ☐ No ☐

Details: ______________________________

____

Duty Psychiatrist

Name of Duty Psychiatrist: ______________________________

Date seen: ______________________________

Assessed: Yes ☐ No ☐ Details: __________

____

S.35 Admission Yes ☐ No ☐

Comments relating to bail: ______________________________

____

Available care/suggested bail conditions

This information has been verified and the care detailed is available

1. Defendant to reside at: ______________________________

   ____

2. Day care/support: Yes ☐ No ☐ Details ☐

   ____

   ____

3. Psychiatric outpatient appointment: Yes ☐ No ☐

   Details: ______________________________________

   ____

   ____

This information has been collected by the Diversion from Custody Project Worker and/or Duty Psychiatrist through an interview with the defendant and through other enquiries with the prior consent of the defendant. It is provided to the Court, CPS and the defence. If any further information is required please contact:

____

Signed: ....

Date: ....

Appendix IV

MODEL JOB DESCRIPTION

1. **Introduction**
   Background and history of project. Funding availability and duration.

2. **Duties and responsibilities**
   a) To divert mentally disordered offenders from prosecution by:
      (i) Assessing them in police custody, or on remand in prison, or on remand on bail.
      and
      (ii) By providing information to the police and Crown Prosecution Service of the nature and severity of the mental disorder, to facilitate a decision by the police not to charge or by the Crown Prosecution Service to discontinue prosecution.

   b) To divert mentally disordered offenders from remand to custody by:
      (i) Liaising with local psychiatric services to enable psychiatric assessments to be undertaken prior to first appearance in Court.
      (ii) Liaising with social services, probation and housing agencies to arrange suitable accommodation to enable a mentally disordered offender to be remanded on bail.
      (iii) Liaising with local psychiatric services on admission to hospital as a voluntary patient.
      (iv) Liaising with local psychiatric services for admission to hospital under sections 2, 3, 4 or 35 as appropriate as an alternative to a remand in custody where a serious offence is charged.
      (v) To ensure the provision of a bail support package for mentally disordered offenders to help reduce the risk of breach of bail conditions.

c) To reduce the number of mentally disordered offenders serving custodial sentences by:
   (i) Liaising with probation on preparation of pre-sentence reports to facilitate a non-custodial sentence e.g. probation order with conditions of residence or treatment.
   (ii) Liaising with local psychiatric services or other secure facilities as appropriate to facilitate the making of a hospital order under S37 or S38 MHA as appropriate.
   (iii) Liaising with the appropriate local psychiatric hospital or regional secure unit, or special hospital and Home Office C3 Division, to facilitate transfer to hospital under S47 Mental Health Act.

d) To reduce the risk of re-offending by:
   (i) Liaising with social services, health authority and probation service to provide an appropriate package of after-care and support to enable a successful return to the community and prevent re-offending.
   (ii) Liaising with housing providers to obtain appropriate housing for the mentally disordered offender.

e) To keep appropriate records.

f) To provide specialist advice and support to other agencies with responsibility for providing health and social care and housing for mentally disordered offenders.

3. Management and support

(insert details)

4. Summary of conditions of service

(insert details)

5. Qualifications and qualities

Essential

a) Qualified Probation Officer/Community Psychiatric Nurse/Approved Social Worker.
b) Thorough knowledge of the Mental Health Act 1983, Bail Act 1976, Police and Criminal Evidence Act 1984 and relevant Codes of Practice.
c) The ability to communicate effectively orally and in writing.
d) Experience of working with mentally disordered offenders.

Desirable

a) Sound organisational skills.
b) Self-motivation and the ability to motivate others.
c) Energy, drive and enthusiasm.
d) Adaptability and flexibility.

Appendix V

USEFUL ADDRESSES

Mental Health Foundation
8 Hallam Street
LONDON W1N 6DH

Good Practices in Mental Health
380–384 Harrow Road
LONDON W9 2HU

Home Office C3 Division
Queen Anne's Gate
LONDON SW1H 9AT

National MIND and National MIND Publications
Granta House
15–19 Broadway
Stratford
LONDON E15 4BQ

Department of Health
Wellington House
133–155 Waterloo Road
LONDON SE1 8UG

Institute of Psychiatrists
De Crespigny Park
Denmark Hill
LONDON SE26

HM Prison Service Headquarters
Cleland House
Page Street
LONDON SW1P 4LN

NACRO
169 Clapham Road
LONDON SW9 OPU

National Association of Voluntary Hostels
Fulham Palace
Bishops Avenue
LONDON SW6 6EA

Kings Fund College
2 Palace Court
LONDON W2 4HS

Appendix VI

Guidelines and procedures

Suggested contents

a) Introduction — history and background.

b) Role of Forum — delegation of responsibility for matters relating to mentally disordered offenders.

   (i) Aims and objectives
   (ii) Status
   (iii) Membership
   (iv) Function
   (v) Service provision

c) Definitions — e.g. mentally disordered offenders.

d) Recognition — issues relating to recognition of mental illness and learning disability.

e) Legal framework — abstracts of (i) legislation and (ii) codes of practice, of non-statutory guidance.

f) (i) Agency procedures
   (ii) Job titles
   (iii) Functions and responsibilities

g) Multi-agency management.
   (i) Introduction
   (ii) Principles
   (iii) Diversion schemes — operation and management arrangements for each local scheme if more than one

h) Monitoring — statistics and activity levels.
   — delivered quarterly.

i) Evaluation — regular annual programme.

j) Review — identifying gaps etc. at regular intervals.

k) Agencies represented.

Appendix VII

Model remit for diversion forum

1. Title:

2. Frequency of meetings — quarterly including an AGM at which a Chair will be elected.

3. Membership

   a) Representatives of all the agencies involved in the criminal justice system.

   b) Representatives of agencies responsible for commissioning or providing health and social care for mentally disordered offenders.

4. Purpose

   a) To discuss all issues relating to mentally disordered offenders in the criminal justice system in (area).

   b) To identify issues and make recommendations on improvements to existing services and development of new services to facilitate diversion from custody.

   c) To monitor and evaluate multi-agency services and service development.

   d) To develop and maintain guidelines and procedures to be agreed, adopted and adhered to by each relevant agency in order to establish a clear understanding of the roles and responsibilities of each agency in relation to mentally disordered offenders.

Appendix VIII

Mental Health Act 1983

Section 2, 3, 7, 35, 36, 37, 41, 44, 47, 48, 117, 136

PART II

COMPULSORY
ADMISSION TO HOSPITAL AND GUARDIANSHIP

Procedure for hospital admission

2.—(1) A patient may be admitted to a hospital and detained there for the period allowed by subsection (4) below in pursuance of an application (in this Act referred to as "an application for admission for assessment") made in accordance with sub-sections (2) and (3) below.

(2) An application for admission for assessment may be made in respect of a patient on the grounds that—

(*a*) he is suffering from mental disorder of a nature or degree which warrants the detention of the patient in a hospital for assessment (or for assessment followed by medical treatment) for at least a limited period; and

(*b*) he ought to be so detained in the interests of his own health or safety or with a view to the protection of other persons.

(3) An application for admission for assessment shall be founded on the written recommendations in the prescribed form of two registered medical practitioners, including in each case a statement that in the opinion of the practitioner the conditions set out in subsection (2) above are complied with.

(4) Subject to the provisions of section 29(4) below, a patient admitted to hospital in pursuance of an application for admission for assessment may be detained for a period not exceeding 28 days beginning with the day on which he is admitted, but shall not be detained after the expiration of that period unless before it has expired he has become liable to be detained by virtue of a subsequent application, order or direction under the following provisions of this Act.

3.—(1) A patient may be admitted to a hospital and detained there for the period allowed by the following provisions of this Act in pursuance of an application (in this Act referred to as "an application for admission for treatment") made in accordance with this section.

(2) An application for admission for treatment may be made in respect of a patient on the grounds that—

(*a*) he is suffering from mental illness, severe mental impairment, psychopathic disorder or mental impairment and his mental disorder is of a nature or degree which makes it appropriate for him to receive medical treatment in a hospital; and

(*b*) in the case of psychopathic disorder or mental impairment, such treatment is likely to alleviate or prevent a deterioration of his condition; and

(*c*) it is necessary for the health or safety of the patient or for the protection of other persons that he should receive such treatment and it cannot be provided unless he is detained under this section.

(3) An application for admission for treatment shall be founded on the written recommendations in the prescribed form of two registered medical practitioners, including in each case a statement that in the opinion of the practitioner the conditions set out in subsection (2) above are complied with; and each such recommendation shall include—

(*a*) such particulars as may be prescribed of the grounds for that opinion so far as it relates to the conditions set out in paragraphs (*a*) and (*b*) of that subsection; and

(*b*) a statement of the reasons for that opinion so far as it relates to the conditions set out in paragraph (*c*) of that subsection, specifying whether other methods of dealing with the patient are available and, if so, why they are not appropriate.

Guardianship

7.—(1) A patient who has attained the age of 16 years may be received into guardianship, for the period allowed by the following provisions of this Act, in pursuance of an application (in this Act referred to as "a guardianship application") made in accordance with this section.

(2) A guardianship application may be made in respect of a patient on the grounds that—

(*a*) he is suffering from mental disorder, being mental illness, severe mental impairment, psychopathic disorder or mental impairment and his mental disorder is of a nature or degree which warrants his reception into guardianship under this section; and

(*b*) it is necessary in the interests of the welfare of the patient or for the protection of other persons that the patient should be so received.

(3) A guardianship application shall be founded on the written recommendations in the prescribed form of two registered medical practitioners, including in each case a statement that in the opinion of the practitioner the conditions set out in subsection (2) above are complied with; and each such recommendation shall include—

(*a*) such particulars as may be prescribed of the grounds for that opinion so far as it relates to the conditions set out in paragraph (*a*) of that subsection; and

(*b*) a statement of the reasons for that opinion so far as it relates to the conditions set out in paragraph (*b*) of that subsection.

(4) A guardianship application shall state the age of the patient or, if his exact age is not known to the applicant, shall state (if it be the fact) that the patient is believed to have attained the age of 16 years.

(5) The person named as guardian in a guardianship application may be either a local social services authority or any other person (including the applicant himself); but a guardianship application in which a person other than a local social services authority is named as guardian shall be of no effect unless it is accepted on behalf of that person by the local social services authority for the area in which he resides, and shall be accompanied by a statement in writing by that person that he is willing to act as guardian.

PART III

PATIENTS CONCERNED IN CRIMINAL PROCEEDINGS OR UNDER SENTENCE

Remands to hospital

35.—(1) Subject to the provisions of this section, the Crown Court or a magistrates' court may remand an accused person to a hospital specified by the court for a report on his mental condition.

(2) For the purposes of this section an accused person is—

(*a*) in relation to the Crown Court, any person who is awaiting trial before the court for an offence punishable with imprisonment or who has been arraigned before the court for such an offence and has not yet been sentenced or otherwise dealt with for the offence on which he has been arraigned;

(*b*) in relation to a magistrates' court, any person who has been convicted by the court of an offence punishable on summary conviction with imprisonment and any person charged with such an offence if the court is satisfied that he did the act or made the omission charged or he has consented to the exercise by the court of the powers conferred by this section.

(3) Subject to subsection (4) below, the powers conferred by this section may be exercised if—

(*a*) the court is satisfied, on the written or oral evidence of a registered medical practitioner, that there is reason to suspect that the accused person is suffering from mental illness, psychopathic disorder, severe mental impairment or mental impairment; and

(*b*) the court is of the opinion that it would be impracticable for a report on his mental condition to be made if he were remanded on bail;

but those powers shall not be exercised by the Crown Court in respect of a person who has been convicted before the court if the sentence for the offence of which he has been convicted is fixed by law.

(4) The court shall not remand an accused person to a hospital under this section unless satisfied, on the written or oral evidence of the registered medical practitioner who would be responsible for making the report or of some other person representing the managers of the hospital, that arrangements have been made for his admission to that hospital and for his admission to it within the period of seven days beginning with the date of the remand; and if the court is so satisfied it may, pending his admission, give directions for his conveyance to and detention in a place of safety.

(5) Where a court has remanded an accused person under this section it may further remand him if it appears to the court, on the written or oral evidence of the registered medical practitioner responsible for making the report, that a further

remand is necessary for completing the assessment of the accused person's mental condition.

(6) The power of further remanding an accused person under this section may be exercised by the court without his being brought before the court if he is represented by counsel or a solicitor and his counsel or solicitor is given an opportunity of being heard.

(7) An accused person shall not be remanded or further remanded under this section for more than 28 days at a time or for more than 12 weeks in all; and the court may at any time terminate the remand if it appears to the court that it is appropriate to do so.

(8) An accused person remanded to hospital under this section shall be entitled to obtain at his own expense an independent report on his mental condition from a registered medical practitioner chosen by him and to apply to the court on the basis of it for his remand to be terminated under subsection (7) above.

(9) Where an accused person is remanded under this section—

(*a*) a constable or any other person directed to do so by the court shall convey the accused person to the hospital specified by the court within the period mentioned in subsection (4) above; and

(*b*) the managers of the hospital shall admit him within that period and thereafter detain him in accordance with the provisions of this section.

(10) If an accused person absconds from a hospital to which he has been remanded under this section, or while being conveyed to or from that hospital, he may be arrested without warrant by any constable and shall, after being arrested, be brought as soon as practicable before the court that remanded him; and the court may thereupon terminate the remand and deal with him in any way in which it could have dealt with him if he had not been remanded under this section.

36.—(1) Subject to the provisions of this section, the Crown Court may, instead of remanding an accused person in custody, remand him to a hospital specified by the court if satisfied, on the written or oral evidence of two registered medical practitioners, that he is suffering from mental illness or severe mental impairment of a nature or degree which makes it appropriate for him to be detained in a hospital for medical treatment.

(2) For the purposes of this section an accused person is any person who is in custody awaiting trial before the Crown Court for an offence punishable with imprisonment (other than an offence the sentence for which is fixed by law) or who at any time before sentence is in custody in the course of a trial before that court for such an offence.

(3) The court shall not remand an accused person under this section to a hospital unless it is satisfied, on the written or oral evidence of the registered medical practitioner who would be in charge of his treatment or of some other person representing the managers of the hospital, that arrangements have been made for his admission to that hospital and for his admission to it within the period of seven days beginning with the date of the remand; and if the court is so satisfied it may, pending his admission, give directions for his conveyance to and detention in a place of safety.

(4) Where a court has remanded an accused person under this section it may further remand him if it appears to the court, on the written or oral evidence of the responsible medical officer, that a further remand is warranted.

(5) The power of further remanding an accused person under this section may be exercised by the court without his being brought before the court if he is represented by counsel or a solicitor and his counsel or solicitor is given an opportunity of being heard.

(6) An accused person shall not be remanded or further remanded under this section for more than 28 days at a time or for more than 12 weeks in all; and the court may at any time terminate the remand if it appears to the court that it is appropriate to do so.

(7) An accused person remanded to hospital under this section shall be entitled to obtain at his own expense an independent report on his mental condition from a registered medical practitioner chosen by him and to apply to the court on the basis of it for his remand to be terminated under subsection (6) above.

(8) Subsections (9) and (10) of section 35 above shall have effect in relation to a remand under this section as they have effect in relation to a remand under that section.

Hospital and guardianship orders

37.—(1) Where a person is convicted before the Crown Court of an offence punishable with imprisonment other than an offence the sentence for which is fixed by law, or is convicted by a magistrates' court of an offence punishable on summary conviction with imprisonment, and the conditions mentioned in subsection (2) below are satisfied, the court may by order authorise his admission to and detention in such hospital as may be specified in the order or, as the case may be, place him under the guardianship of a local social services authority or of such other person approved by a local social services authority as may be so specified.

(2) The conditions referred to in subsection (1) above are that—

(*a*) the court is satisfied, on the written or oral evidence of two registered medical practitioners, that the offender is suffering from mental illness, psychopathic disorder, severe mental impairment or mental impairment and that either—

(i) the mental disorder from which the offender is suffering is of a nature or degree which makes it appropriate for him to be detained in a hospital for medical treatment and, in the case of psychopathic disorder or mental impairment, that such treatment is likely to alleviate or prevent a deterioration of his condition; or

(ii) in the case of an offender who has attained the age of 16 years, the mental disorder is of a nature or degree which warrants his reception into guardianship under this Act; and

(*b*) the court is of the opinion, having regard to all the circumstances including the nature of the offence and the character and antecedents of the offender, and to the other available methods of dealing with him, that the most suitable method of disposing of the case is by means of an order under this section.

(3) Where a person is charged before a magistrates' court with any act or omission as an offence and the court would have power, on convicting him of

that offence, to make an order under subsection (1) above in his case as being a person suffering from mental illness or severe mental impairment, then, if the court is satisfied that the accused did the act or made the omission charged, the court may, if it thinks fit, make such an order without convicting him.

(4) An order for the admission of an offender to a hospital (in this Act referred to as "a hospital order") shall not be made under this section unless the court is satisfied on the written or oral evidence of the registered medical practitioner who would be in charge of his treatment or of some other person representing the managers of the hospital that arrangements have been made for his admission to that hospital in the event of such an order being made by the court, and for his admission to it within the period of 28 days beginning with the date of the making of such an order; and the court may, pending his admission within that period, give such directions as it thinks fit for his conveyance to and detention in a place of safety.

(5) If within the said period of 28 days it appears to the Secretary of State that by reason of an emergency or other special circumstances it is not practicable for the patient to be received into the hospital specified in the order, he may give directions for the admission of the patient to such other hospital as appears to be appropriate instead of the hospital so specified; and where such directions are given—

(*a*) the Secretary of State shall cause the person having the custody of the patient to be informed, and

(*b*) the hospital order shall have effect as if the hospital specified in the directions were substituted for the hospital specified in the order.

(6) An order placing an offender under the guardianship of a local social services authority or of any other person (in this Act referred to as "a guardianship order") shall not be made under this section unless the court is satisfied that that authority or person is willing to receive the offender into guardianship.

(7) A hospital order or guardianship order shall specify the form or forms of mental disorder referred to in subsection (2)(*a*) above from which, upon the evidence taken into account under that subsection, the offender is found by the court to be suffering; and no such order shall be made unless the offender is described by each of the practitioners whose evidence is taken into account under that subsection as suffering from the same one of those forms of mental disorder, whether or not he is also described by either of them as suffering from another of them.

(8) Where an order is made under this section, the court shall not pass sentence of imprisonment or impose a fine or make a probation order in respect of the offence or make any such order as is mentioned in paragraph (*b*) or (*c*) of section 7(7) of the Children and Young Persons Act 1969 in respect of the offender, but may make any other order which the court has power to make apart from this section; and for the purposes of this subsection "sentence of imprisonment" includes any sentence or order for detention.

Restriction orders

41.—(1) Where a hospital order is made in respect of an offender by the Crown Court, and it appears to the court, having regard to the nature of the offence, the antecedents of the offender and the risk of his committing further offences if set at large, that it is necessary for the protection of the public from serious harm so to do, the court may, subject to the provisions of this section, further order that the offender shall be subject to the special restrictions set out in this section, either without limit of time or during such period as may be specified in the order; and an order under this section shall be known as "a restriction order".

(2) A restriction order shall not be made in the case of any person unless at least one of the registered medical practitioners whose evidence is taken into account by the court under section 37(2)(*a*) above has given evidence orally before the court.

(3) The special restrictions applicable to a patient in respect of whom a restriction order is in force are as follows—

(*a*) none of the provisions of Part II of this Act relating to the duration, renewal and expiration of authority for the detention of patients shall apply, and the patient shall continue to be liable to be detained by virtue of the relevant hospital order until he is duly discharged under the said Part II or absolutely discharged under section 42, 73, 74 or 75 below;

(*b*) no application shall be made to a Mental Health Review Tribunal in respect of a patient under section 66 or 69(1) below;

(*c*) the following powers shall be exercisable only with the consent of the Secretary of State, namely—

(i) power to grant leave of absence to the patient under section 17 above;

(ii) power to transfer the patient in pursuance of regulations under section 19 above; and

(iii) power to order the discharge of the patient under section 23 above;

and if leave of absence is granted under the said section 17 power to recall the patient under that section shall vest in the Secretary of State as well as the responsible medical officer; and

(*d*) the power of the Secretary of State to recall the patient under the said section 17 and power to take the patient into custody and return him under section 18 above may be exercised at any time;

and in relation to any such patient section 40(4) above shall have effect as if it referred to Part II of Schedule 1 to this Act instead of Part I of that Schedule.

(4) A hospital order shall not cease to have effect under section 40(5) above if a restriction order in respect of the patient is in force at the material time.

(5) Where a restriction order in respect of a patient ceases to have effect while the relevant hospital order continues in force, the provisions of section 40 above and Part I of Schedule 1 to this Act shall apply to the patient as if he had been admitted to the hospital in pursuance of a hospital order (without a restriction order) made on the date on which the restriction order ceased to have effect.

(6) While a person is subject to a restriction order the responsible medical officer shall at such intervals (not exceeding one year) as the Secretary of State may direct examine and report to the Secretary of State on that person; and every report shall contain such particulars as the Secretary of State may require.

44.—(1) Where an offender is committed under section 43(1) above and the magistrates' court by which he is committed is satisfied on written or oral evidence that arrangements have been made for the admission of the offender to a hospital in the event of an order being made under this section, the court may, instead of committing him in custody, by order direct him to be admitted to that hospital, specifying it, and to be detained there until the case is disposed of by the Crown

Court, and may give such directions as it thinks fit for his production from the hospital to attend the Crown Court by which his case is to be dealt with.

(2) The evidence required by subsection (1) above shall be given by the registered medical practitioner who would be in charge of the offender's treatment or by some other person representing the managers of the hospital in question.

(3) The power to give directions under section 37(4) above, section 37(5) above and section 40(1) above shall apply in relation to an order under this section as they apply in relation to a hospital order, but as if references to the period of 28 days mentioned in section 40(1) above were omitted; and subject as aforesaid an order under this section shall, until the offender's case is disposed of by the Crown Court, have the same effect as a hospital order together with a restriction order, made without limitation of time.

Transfer to hospital of prisoners, etc.

47.—(1) If in the case of a person serving a sentence of imprisonment the Secretary of State is satisfied, by reports from at least two registered medical practitioners—

(*a*) that the said person is suffering from mental illness, psychopathic disorder, severe mental impairment or mental impairment; and

(*b*) that the mental disorder from which that person is suffering is of a nature or degree which makes it appropriate for him to be detained in a hospital for medical treatment and, in the case of psychopathic disorder or mental impairment, that such treatment is likely to alleviate or prevent a deterioration of his condition;

the Secretary of State may, if he is of the opinion having regard to the public interest and all the circumstances that it is expedient so to do, by warrant direct that that person be removed to and detained in such hospital (not being a mental nursing home) as may be specified in the direction; and a direction under this section shall be known as "a transfer direction".

(2) A transfer direction shall cease to have effect at the expiration of the period of 14 days beginning with the date on which it is given unless within that period the person with respect to whom it was given has been received into the hospital specified in the direction.

(3) A transfer direction with respect to any person shall have the same effect as a hospital order made in his case.

(4) A transfer direction shall specify the form or forms of mental disorder referred to in paragraph (*a*) of subsection (1) above from which, upon the reports taken into account under that subsection, the patient is found by the Secretary of State to be suffering; and no such direction shall be given unless the patient is described in each of those reports as suffering from the same form of disorder, whether or not he is also described in either of them as suffering from another form.

(5) References in this Part of this Act to a person serving a sentence of imprisonment include references—

(*a*) to a person detained in pursuance of any sentence or order for detention made by a court in criminal proceedings (other than an order under any enactment to which section 46 above applies);

(*b*) to a person committed to custody under section 115(3) of the Magistrates' Courts Act 1980 (which relates to persons who fail to comply with an order to enter into recognisances to keep the peace or be of good behaviour); and

(*c*) to a person committed by a court to a prison or other institution to which the Prison Act 1952 applies in default of payment of any sum adjudged to be paid on his conviction.

48.—(1) If in the case of a person to whom this section applies the Secretary of State is satisfied by the same reports as are required for the purposes of section 47 above that that person is suffering from mental illness or severe mental impairment of a nature or degree which makes it appropriate for him to be detained in a hospital for medical treatment and that he is in urgent need of such treatment, the Secretary of State shall have the same power of giving a transfer direction in respect of him under that section as if he were serving a sentence of imprisonment.

(2) This section applies to the following persons, that is to say—

(*a*) persons detained in a prison or remand centre, not being persons serving a sentence of imprisonment or persons falling within the following paragraphs of this subsection;

(*b*) persons remanded in custody by a magistrates' court;

(*c*) civil prisoners, that is to say, persons committed by a court to prison for a limited term (including persons committed to prison in pursuance of a writ of attachment), who are not persons falling to be dealt with under section 47 above;

(*d*) persons detained under the Immigration Act 1971.

(3) Subsections (2) to (4) of section 47 above shall apply for the purposes of this section and of any transfer direction given by virtue of this section as they apply for the purposes of that section and of any transfer direction under that section.

After-care

117.—(1) This section applies to persons who are detained under section 3 above, or admitted to a hospital in pursuance of a hospital order made under section 37 above, or transferred to a hospital in pursuance of a transfer direction made under section 47 or 48 above, and then cease to be detained and leave hospital.

(2) It shall be the duty of the District Health Authority and of the local social services authority to provide, in co-operation with relevant voluntary agencies, after-care services for any person to whom this section applies until such time as the District Health Authority and the local social services authority are satisfied that the person concerned is no longer in need of such services.

(3) In this section "the District Health Authority" means the District Health Authority for the district, and "the local social services authority" means the local social services authority for the area in which the person concerned is resident or to which he is sent on discharge by the hospital in which he was detained.

136.—(1) If a constable finds in a place to which the public have access a person who appears to him to be suffering from mental disorder and to be in immediate need of care or control, the constable may, if he thinks it necessary to do so in the interests of that person or for the protection of other persons, remove that person to a place of safety within the meaning of section 135 above.

(2) A person removed to a place of safety under this section may be detained there for a period not exceeding 72 hours for the purpose of enabling him to be examined by a registered medical practitioner and to be interviewed by an approved social worker and of making any necessary arrangements for his treatment or care.

Appendix IX

Mental Health Act 1983

Code of Practice

(a) pp. 16–19 (b) pp. 53–59 (c) pp. 72–73

Part III of the Mental Health Act — patients concerned with criminal proceedings (pp. 16–19)

Assessment

General

Responsibility to patients

3.1 Those subject to criminal proceedings have the same right to psychiatric assessment and treatment as other citizens. The aim should be to ensure that everyone in prison or police custody in need of medical treatment for mental disorder which can only satisfactorily be given in a hospital as defined by the Act is admitted to such a hospital.

3.2 All professionals involved in the operation of Part III of the Act should remember:

a. the vulnerability of people, especially those who are mentally disordered, when in police or prison custody. The risk of suicide or other self destructive behaviour should be of special concern;

b. that a prison hospital is not a hospital within the meaning of the Act. Treatment facilities are limited, and the provisions of Part IV of the Act do not apply.

Individual professional responsibilities

3.3 All professionals concerned with the operation of Part III of the Act should be familiar with:

— the relevant provisions of the Act and paragraphs of the Memorandum (paras 115 to 188);

— any relevant guidance issued by or under the auspices of the Home Office including that in Home Office Circular 66/90 and E L(90)168, on Provision for Mentally Disordered Offenders;

— the responsibilities of their own and other disciplines and authorities and agencies;

— available facilities and services.

Agency responsibility

3.4 Regional health authorities in England and district health authorities in Wales should:

a. be able to provide to any requesting court in compliance with section 39 of the Act, and also in response to any other proper request, up-to-date and full information on the range of facilities for a potential patient in hospitals, including secure facilities. Facilities to which the patient might be admitted outside their district or region may need to be specified and the arrangements for their funding clarified;

b. appoint a named person to respond to these requests.

3.5 Section 27 of the Criminal Justice Act 1991 added a new section 39A to the Act which requires a local social services authority to inform the court if it or any other person is willing to receive the offender into guardianship and, if so, to provide such information as it reasonably can about how the guardian's powers can be expected to be exercised.

3.6 Local authorities should appoint a named person to respond to requests from the courts for them to consider the making of guardianship orders.

Assessment by a doctor

3.7 Where a doctor is asked to provide an opinion in relation to a possible admission under Part III of the Act:

a. he should identify himself to the person being assessed, and explain at whose request he is preparing his report, discussing any implications this may have for confidentiality;

b. he should have access to relevant social enquiry reports, the inmate's medical record (where the defendant is remanded in prison custody) and previous psychiatric treatment records as well as relevant documentation regarding the alleged offence. If he is not given any of this information he should say so clearly in his report (see paras 2.6 and 2.35).

Where a doctor had previously treated the person it may be desirable for him to prepare the report. It would also be desirable for the doctor (or one of them if two doctors are preparing reports) to have appropriate beds at his disposal or where necessary to take responsibility for referring the case to another doctor with access to such facilities.

3.8 The doctor should where possible make contact with independent information about the person's previous history, previous psychiatric treatment and patterns of behaviour.

3.9 Any assessment of the person is a medical responsibility. Appropriate members of the clinical team who would be involved with the individual's care and treatment may also be involved. It is often desirable for a nurse (who will be able to undertake a nursing assessment of the person's needs for nursing care and treatment and advise on whether he can be managed in the hospital) to accompany the assessing doctor where admission to hospital is likely to be recommended. The doctor should make contact with the social worker or probation officer who is preparing a social enquiry report, especially when psychiatric treatment is suggested as a condition of a probation order.

3.10 The doctor should not in his report anticipate the outcome of proceedings to establish guilt or innocence. It is sometimes appropriate to advise that a further report should be submitted to court after conviction and before sentencing. In any report prepared before a verdict is reached, the doctor may give advice on the appropriate disposal of the person in the event that he is convicted.

3.11 When the doctor has concluded that the person needs treatment in hospital, but there is no facility available, the task is not completed until:

a. details of the type of provision required have been forwarded in writing to the district health authority, who will need detailed advice in order to discharge their responsibilities;

b. in suitable cases contact has been made with the local NHS forensic psychiatrist.

Role of ASW

3.12 If an ASW has to be called to the prison or to a court to see a prisoner about to be released, with a view to making an application for admission as a detained patient under sections 2 or 3, as much advance warning as possible should be given, and the ASW must be given ample time and facilities for interviewing the prisoner. The ASW should be given access to the social inquiry report as it is difficult within the confines of a prison/court to assess how a prisoner (convicted or on remand) might be able to benefit from alternative treatment in the community.

Transfer of prisoners to hospital

3.13 The need for in-patient treatment for a prisoner must be identified and acted on swiftly, and contact made urgently between the prison doctor and the hospital doctor. The Home Office must be advised on the urgency of the need for transfer.

3.14 The transfer of a prisoner to hospital under the Act should not be delayed until close to his release date. A transfer in such circumstances may well be seen by the prisoner as being primarily intended to extend his detention and result in an unco-operative attitude towards treatment.

15 Medical treatment (pp. 53–59)

(*Paras 189–205 of the Memorandum*)

Introduction

15.1 This chapter, whilst referring to some aspects of the Mental Health Act, is primarily concerned with medical treatment generally and in particular capacity (see paras 15.9–15.11) and consent to treatment (see paras 15.12–15.24).

15.2 Everyone involved in the medical treatment of mental disorder should be familiar with the provisions of Part IV of the Act, related statutory instruments, relevant circulars and advice notes. But it is for the rmo to ensure that there is compliance with the Act's provisions relating to medical treatment.

15.3 The Managers should arrange to monitor compliance with the provisions of Part IV of the Act. (For a more detailed discussion of Part IV of the Act see Chapter 16).

Medical treatment

15.4 For the purposes of the Act, medical treatment includes 'nursing and also includes care, habilitation and rehabilitation under medical supervision', ie the broad range of activities aimed at alleviating or preventing a deterioration of, the patient's mental disorder. It includes physical treatment such as ECT and the administration of drugs, and psychotherapy.

Treatment plans

15.5 Treatment plans are essential for both informal and detained patients. Consultants should co-ordinate the formulation of a treatment plan in consultation with their professional colleagues. The plan should be recorded in the patient's clinical notes.

15.6 A treatment plan should include a description of the immediate and long-term goals for the patient with a clear indication of the treatments proposed and the methods of treatment. The patient's progress and possible changes to the plan should be reviewed at regular intervals.

15.7 Wherever possible the whole plan should be discussed with the patient, with a view to him making his own contribution and saying whether or not he agrees with it. It is also important to discuss it with the appropriate relatives concerned about a patient (but only with his consent in cases where the patient is capable of providing consent).

Capacity and consent to treatment introduction

15.8 In general the common law, as it relates to consent to treatment, applies to all patients, informal or detained. Therefore, valid consent is required from a patient before medical treatment can be given, except where the law (either the common law or statute) provides authority to treat him without consent. The common law may authorise treatment where the patient is incapable of consenting (see paras 15.9–15.11 and 15.16–15.23) or, rarely, even where the patient can consent (see, for one set of circumstances, para 15.24). Statute law may authorise treatment, for example Part IV of the Act (see Chapter 16).

Capacity to make treatment decisions

15.9 The assessment of a patient's capacity to make a decision about his own medical treatment is a matter for clinical judgment, guided by current professional practice and subject to legal requirements. It is the personal responsibility of any doctor proposing to treat a patient to determine whether the patient has capacity to give a valid consent.

Capacity: the basic principles

15.10 An individual in order to have capacity must be able to:

- understand what medical treatment is and that somebody has said that he needs it and why the treatment is being proposed;
- understand in broad terms the nature of the proposed treatment;
- understand its principal benefits and risks;
- understand what will be the consequences of not receiving the proposed treatment;
- possess the capacity to make a choice.

It must be remembered:

- any assessment as to an individual's capacity has to be made in relation to a particular treatment proposal;
- capacity in an individual with a mental disorder can be variable over time and should be assessed at the time the treatment is proposed;
- all assessments of an individual's capacity should be fully recorded in the patient's medical notes.

15.11 A person suffering from a mental disorder is not necessarily incapable of giving consent. Capacity to consent is variable in people with mental disorder and should be assessed in relation to the particular patient, at the particular time, as regards the particular treatment proposed. Not everyone is equally capable of understanding the same explanation of a treatment plan. A person is more likely to be able to give valid consent if the explanation is appropriate to the level of his assessed ability.

Consent; the basic principles

15.12 'Consent' is the voluntary and continuing permission of the patient to receive a particular treatment, based on an adequate knowledge of the purpose, nature, likely effects and risks of that treatment including the likelihood of its success and any alternatives to it. Permission given under any unfair or undue pressure is not 'consent'.

Consent from patients with capacity to consent

15.13 The information which must be given should be related to the particular patient, the particular treatment and the relevant medical knowledge and practice. In every case sufficient information must be given to ensure that the patient understands in broad terms the nature, likely effects and risks of that treatment including the likelihood of its success and any alternatives to it. Additional information is a matter of professional judgment for the doctor proposing the treatment. The patient should be invited to ask questions and the doctor should answer fully, frankly, and truthfully. There may be a compelling reason, in the patient's interest, for not disclosing certain information. A doctor who chooses not to disclose must be prepared to justify the decision. If a doctor chooses not to answer a patient's question he should make this clear so that the patient knows where he stands.

15.14 The patient should be told that his consent to treatment can be withdrawn at any time and that fresh consent is required before further treatment can be given or reinstated. The patient should receive an explanation of the likely consequences of not receiving treatment. (See para 16.15 on withdrawing consent in relation to treatment administered under Part IV of the Act.)

15.15 It is the duty of everyone proposing to give treatment to use reasonable care and skill, not only in giving information prior to seeking a patient's consent but also in meeting the continuing obligation to provide the patient with adequate information about the proposed treatment and alternatives to it.

Treatment of those without capacity to consent

15.16 There are three instances in which a patient who is not capable of giving consent may be treated, which are dealt with in the following paragraphs.

15.17 A patient may be incapable of giving consent because he is an immature child, in which case a parent or person with parental responsibility may consent (see Chapter 30).

15.18 A patient can be given treatment without consent when he is incapable of giving consent because he is unconscious and is in urgent need of treatment to preserve life, health or well-being (unless there is unequivocal and reliable evidence that the patient did not want that treatment), provided that it is necessary that the treatment be administered while the patient is still unconscious.

15.19 A patient can be given treatment without consent when he is incapable of giving consent provided two conditions are satisfied. The first condition is that the patient must lack the capacity (see paras 15.10 and 15.11) *to make a decision and* be in need of medical care. The second condition is that the treatment must be 'in the patient's best interests', which, according to the decision of the House of Lords in *Re F* [1990] 2 A C 1, means that the treatment is:

- necessary to save life or prevent a deterioration or ensure an improvement in the patient's physical or mental health; and

- in accordance with a practice accepted at the time by a responsible body of medical opinion skilled in the particular form of treatment in question (the test that was originally laid down in *Bolam v Friern Hospital Management Committee* [1957] 1 WLR 582).

There are exceptional circumstances in which the proposed treatment should not be carried out on incapable patients without first seeking the approval of the High Court by way of a declaration (see para 15.21). Sterilisation, according to the House of Lords in *Re F* (1990), is one such circumstance.

15.20 The administration of medical treatment to people incapable of taking their own treatment decisions is a matter of much concern to professionals and others involved in their care. It is the personal responsibility of professionals to ensure that they understand the relevant law.

15.21 The procedures to be used when applying for a declaration that a proposed operation for sterilisation is lawful were set out initially by Lord Brandon of Oakbrook in *Re F* and developed by the Official Solicitor in *Practice Note (Official Solicitor: Sterilisation)* [1990] 2 FLR 530. In outline, the procedure is as follows:

i. applications for a declaration that a proposed operation on or medical treatment for a patient can lawfully be carried out despite the inability of such patient to consent thereto should be by way of Originating Summons issuing out of the Family Division of the High Court;

ii. the applicant should normally be the person(s) responsible for the care of the patient or intending to carry out the proposed operation or other treatment, if it is declared to be lawful;

iii. the patient must always be a party and should normally be a respondent. In cases in which the patient is a respondent the patient's guardian ad litem should normally be the Official Solicitor. In any cases in which the Official Solicitor is not either the next friend or the guardian ad litem of the parent or an applicant he shall be respondent;

iv. with a view to protecting the patient's privacy, but subject always to the judge's discretion, the hearing will be in chambers, but the decision and the reasons for that decision will be given in court.

15.22 The *Handbook of Contraceptive Practice* (1990) considers the effect of *Re F* on operations for sterilisation, as well as other matters relating to the sexuality of people with learning disabilities (mental handicap).

15.23 The Law Commission has included a review of aspects of the law relating to mental incapacity in its Fourth Programme of Law Reform (Cm 800). (See *Mentally Incapacitated Adults and Decision-Making: An Overview*, Law Commission Consultation Paper No. 119, HMSO, 1991, and three papers which form the second round of the Law Commission's consultation process: *Mentally Incapacitated Adults and Decision-Making: A New Jurisdiction*, Law Commission Consultation Paper No. 128, *Mentally Incapacitated Adults and Decision Making: Medical Treatment and Research*, Law Commission Consultation Paper No. 129, and *Mentally Incapacitated Adults and Other Vulnerable Adults: Public Law Protection*, Law Commission Consultation Paper No. 130, all HMSO, 1993.)

Treatment of those with capacity to consent where consent is not given

15.24 Ordinarily, a patient capable of giving consent can only be given medical treatment for mental disorder against his wishes in accordance with the provisions of Part IV of the Act. On rare occasions involving emergencies, where it is not possible immediately to apply the provisions of the Mental Health Act, a patient suffering from a mental disorder which is leading to behaviour that is an immediate serious danger to himself or to other people may be given such treatment as represents the minimum necessary response to avert that danger. It must be emphasised that the administration of such treatment is not an alternative to giving treatment under the Mental Health Act to the patient at the earliest opportunity. (see Chapter 18).

17 Part III of the Mental Health Act — patients concerned with criminal proceedings (pp. 72–73)

Treatment and care in hospital

Patients on remand to hospital under sections 35 and 36

17.1 A patient who is remanded to hospital for reports or for treatment is entitled to obtain, at his own expense, an independent report on his medical condition from a registered medical practitioner chosen by him for the purpose of applying to court for the termination of the remand. Managers should help in the exercise of this right.

17.2 The consent to treatment provisions of the Act do not apply to patients remanded under section 35, so in the absence of the patient's consent treatment can only be administered in an emergency under the provisions of the common law. (See Chapter 15).

17.3 Where a patient remanded under section 35 is thought to be in need of medical treatment for mental disorder under Part IV of the Act, the patient should be referred back to court as soon as possible with an appropriate recommendation, and with an assessment of whether the patient is in a fit state to attend court. If there is a delay in securing a court date (for example an order under section 36 can only be made by a Crown Court and there can be a considerable delay before the patient is committed to the Crown Court), and depending on the patient's mental condition, consideration should be given to whether the patient meets the criteria for detention under section 3 of the Act.

17.4 A report prepared in pursuit of a section 35 remand order should contain:

- a statement as to whether a patient is suffering from a specified form of mental disorder as required by the section, identifying its relevance to the alleged offence. The report must not anticipate the outcome of proceedings to establish guilt or innocence, and it may be right to suggest that a further report be submitted to the court between (possible) conviction and sentence;

- relevant social factors;

- any recommendations on care and treatment, including where and when it should take place and who should be responsible.

Information

17.5 The Managers have a duty to give information to the patient's nearest relative (unless the patient objects). This should be exercised with care; while in prison the patient will have been invited to give details of parents or next of kin, but this may not be the 'nearest relative' under the Act.

Appendix X

Police and Criminal Evidence Act 1984

Section 37, 38, 39.

Duties of custody officer before charge

37.—(1) Where
(*a*) a person is arrested for an offence—
(i) without a warrant; or
(ii) under a warrant not endorsed for bail, or
(*b*) a person returns to a police station to answer to bail
the custody officer at each police station where he is detained after his arrest shall determine whether he has before him sufficient evidence to charge that person with the offence for which he was arrested and may detain him at the police station for such period as is necessary to enable him to do so.

(2) If the custody officer determines that he does not have such evidence before him, the person arrested shall be released either on bail or without bail, unless the custody officer has reasonable grounds for believing that his detention without being charged is necessary to secure or preserve evidence relating to an offence for which he is under arrest or to obtain such evidence by questioning him.

(3) If the custody officer has reasonable grounds for so believing, he may authorise the person arrested to be kept in police detention.

(4) Where a custody officer authorises a person who has not been charged to be kept in police detention, he shall, as soon as is practicable, make a written record of the grounds for the detention.

(5) Subject to subsection (6) below, the written record shall be made in the presence of the person arrested who shall at that time be informed by the custody officer of the grounds for his detention.

(6) Subsection (5) above shall not apply where the person arrested is, at the time when the written record is made—
(*a*) incapable of understanding what is said to him;
(*b*) violent or likely to become violent; or
(*c*) in urgent need of medical attention.

(7) Subject to section 41(7) below, if the custody officer determines that he has before him sufficient evidence to charge the person arrested with the offence for which he was arrested, the person arrested—

(*a*) shall be charged; or
(*b*) shall be released without charge, either on bail or without bail.

(8) Where—

(*a*) a person is released under subsection (7)(*b*) above; and
(*b*) at the time of his release a decision whether he should be prosecuted for the offence for which he was arrested has not been taken,

it shall be the duty of the custody officer so to inform him.

(9) If the person arrested is not in a fit state to be dealt with under subsection (7) above, he may be kept in police detention until he is.

(10) The duty imposed on the custody officer under subsection (1) above shall be carried out by him as soon as practicable after the person arrested arrives at the police station or, in the case of a person arrested at the police station, as soon as practicable after the arrest.

(11) Where—

(*a*) an arrested juvenile who was arrested without a warrant is not released under subsection (2) above; and
(*b*) it appears to the custody officer that a decision falls to be taken in pursuance of section 5(2) of the Children and Young Persons Act 1969 whether to lay an information in respect of an offence alleged to have been committed by the arrested juvenile,

it shall be the duty of the custody officer to inform him that such a decision falls to be taken and to specify the offence.

(12) It shall also be the duty of custody officer—

(*a*) to take such steps as are practicable to ascertain the identity of a person responsible for the welfare of the arrested juvenile; and
(*b*) if—
  (i) he ascertains the identify of any such person; and
  (ii) it is practicable to give that person the information which subsection (11) above requires the custody officer to give to the arrested juvenile,

to give that person the information as soon as it is practicable to do so.

(13) For the purposes of subsection (12) above the persons who may be responsible for the welfare of an arrested juvenile are—

(*a*) his parent or guardian; and
(*b*) any other person who has for the time being assumed responsibility for his welfare;

(14) If it appears to the custody officer that a supervision order, as defined in section 11 of the Children and Young Persons Act 1969, is in force in respect of the arrested juvenile, the custody officer shall also give the information to the person responsible for the arrested juvenile's supervision, as soon as it is practicable to do so.

(15) In this Part of this Act—

"arrested juvenile" means a person arrested with or without a warrant who appears to be under the age of 17 and is not excluded from this Part of this Act by section 52 below;

"endorsed for bail" means endorsed with a direction for bail in accordance with section 117(2) of the Magistrates' Courts Act 1980.

Duties of custody officer after charge

38.—(1) Where a person arrested for an offence otherwise than under a warrant endorsed for bail is charged with an offence, the custody officer shall order his release from police detention, either on bail or without bail, unless—

(*a*) if the person arrested is not an arrested juvenile—

(i) his name or address cannot be ascertained or the custody officer has reasonable grounds for doubting whether a name or address furnished by him as his name or address is his real name or address;

(ii) the custody officer has reasonable grounds for believing that the detention of the person arrested is necessary for his own protection or to prevent him from causing physical injury to any other person or from causing loss of or damage to property; or

(iii) the custody officer has reasonable grounds for believing that the person arrested will fail to appear in court to answer to bail or that his detention is necessary to prevent him from interfering with the administration of justice or with the investigation of offences or of a particular offence;

(*b*) if he is an arrested juvenile—

(i) any of the requirements of paragraph (*a*) above is satisfied; or

(ii) the custody officer has reasonable grounds for believing that he ought to be detained in his own interests.

(2) If the release of a person arrested is not required by subsection (1) above, the custody officer may authorise him to be kept in police detention.

(3) Where a custody officer authorises a person who has been charged to be kept in police detention he shall, as soon as practicable, make a written record of the grounds for the detention.

(4) Subject to subsection (5) below the written record shall be made in the presence of the person charged who shall at that time be informed by the custody officer of the grounds for his detention.

(5) Subsection (4) above shall not apply where the person charged is, at the time when the written record is made—

(*a*) incapable of understanding what is said to him;

(*b*) violent or likely to become violent; or

(*c*) in urgent need of medical attention.

(6) Where a custody officer authorises an arrested juvenile to be kept in police detention under subsection (1) above, the custody officer shall, unless he certifies that it is impracticable to do so, make arrangements for the arrested juvenile to be taken into the care of a local authority and detained by the authority, and it shall be lawful to detain him in pursuance of the arrangements.

(7) A certificate made under subsection (6) above in respect of an arrested juvenile shall be produced to the court before which he is first brought thereafter.

(8) In this Part of this Act "local authority" has the same meaning as in the Children and Young Persons Act 1969.

Responsibilities in relation to persons detained

39.—(1) Subject to subsections (2) and (4) below, it shall be the duty of the custody officer at a police station to ensure—

(*a*) that all persons in police detention at that station are treated in accordance with this Act and any code of practice issued under it and relating to the treatment of persons in police detention; and

(*b*) that all matters relating to such persons which are required by this Act or by such codes of practice to be recorded are recorded in the custody records relating to such persons.

(2) If the custody officer, in accordance with any code of practice issued under this Act, transfers or permits the transfer of a person in police detention

(*a*) to the custody of a police officer investigating an offence for which that person is in police detention;

(*b*) to the custody of an officer who has charge of that person outside the police station,

the custody officer shall cease in relation to that person to be subject to the duty imposed on him by subsection (1)(*a*) above; and it shall be the duty of the officer to whom the transfer is made to ensure that he is treated in accordance with the provisions of this Act and of any such codes of practice as are mentioned in subsection (1) above.

(3) If the person detained is subsequently returned to the custody of the custody officer, it shall be the duty of the officer investigating the offence to report to the custody officer as to the manner in which this section and the codes of practice have been complied with while that person was in his custody.

(4) If an arrested juvenile is transferred to the care of a local authority in pursuance of arrangements made under section 38(6) above, the custody officer shall cease in relation to that person to be subject to the duty imposed on him by subsection (1) above.

(5) It shall be the duty of a local authority to make available to an arrested juvenile who is in the authority's care in pursuance of such arrangements such advice and assistance as may be appropriate in the circumstances.

(6) Where—

(*a*) an officer of higher rank than the custody officer gives directions relating to a person in police detention; and

(*b*) the directions are at variance—

(i) with any decision made or action taken by the custody officer in the performance of a duty imposed on him under this Part of this Act; or

(ii) with any decision or action which would but for the directions have been made or taken by him in the performance of such a duty,

the custody officer shall refer the matter at once to an officer of the rank of superintendent or above who is responsible for the police station for which the custody officer is acting as custody officer.

Appendix XI

Police and Criminal Evidence Act 1984

Code of Practice Code C Annexe E

ANNEX E

Summary of provisions relating to mentally disordered and mentally handicapped persons

1. If an officer has any suspicion or is told in good faith that a person of any age, whether or not in custody, may be suffering from mental disorder or mentally handicapped, or cannot understand the significance of questions put to him or his replies, then he shall be treated as a mentally disordered or mentally handicapped person. (See paragraph 1.4)

2. In the case of a person who is mentally disordered or mentally handicapped "the appropriate adult" means:

(a) a relative, guardian or some other person responsible for his care or custody;
(b) someone who has experience of dealing with mentally disordered or mentally handicapped persons but is not a police officer or employed by the police; or
(c) failing either of the above, some other responsible adult aged 18 or over who is not a police officer or employed by the police. (See paragraph 1.7(b))

3. If the custody officer authorises the detention of a person who is mentally handicapped or is suffering from a mental disorder he must as soon as practicable inform the appropriate adult of the grounds for the person's detention and his whereabouts, and ask the adult to come to the police station to see the person. If the appropriate adult is already at the police station when information is given as required in paragraphs 3.1 to 3.4 the information must be given to the detained person in his presence. If the appropriate adult is not at the police station when the information is given then the information must be given to the detained person again in the presence of the appropriate adult once that person arrives. (See paragraphs 3.9 and 3.11)

4. If the appropriate adult, having been informed of the right to legal advice, considers that legal advice should be taken, the provisions of section 6 of the Code apply as if the mentally disordered or mentally handicapped person had requested access to legal advice. (See paragraph 3.13)

5. If a person brought to a police station appears to be suffering from a mental disorder, or is incoherent other than through drunkenness alone, or if a detained person subsequently appears to be mentally disordered, the custody officer must immediately call the police surgeon or, in urgent cases, send the person to *hospital*

or call the nearest available medical practitioner. It is not intended that these provisions should delay the transfer of a person to a place of safety under section 136 of the Mental Health Act 1983 where that is applicable. When an assessment made under that Act is to take place at the police station, the custody officer has discretion not to call the police surgeon so long as he believes that the assessment by a registered medical practitioner can be undertaken without undue delay. (See paragraph 9.2)

6. It is imperative that a mentally disordered or mentally handicapped person who has been detained under section 136 of the Mental Health Act 1983 should be assessed as soon as possible. If that assessment is to take place at the police station, an approved social worker and a registered medical practitioner should be called to the police station as soon as possible in order to interview and examine the person. Once the person has been interviewed and examined and suitable arrangements have been made for his treatment or care, he can no longer be detained under section 136. The person should not be released until he has been seen by both the approved social worker and the registered medical practitioner. (See paragraph 3.10)

7. If a mentally disordered or mentally handicapped person is cautioned in the absence of the appropriate adult, the caution must be repeated in the adult's presence. (See paragraph 10.6)

8. A mentally disordered or mentally handicapped person must not be interviewed or asked to provide or sign a written statement in the absence of the appropriate adult unless an officer of the rank of superintendent or above considers that delay will involve an immediate risk of harm to persons or serious loss of or serious damage to property. Questioning in these circumstances may not continue in the absence of the appropriate adult once sufficient information to avert the risk has been obtained. A record shall be made of the grounds for any decision to begin an interview in these circumstances. (See paragraph 11.14 and Annex C)

9. Where the appropriate adult is present at an interview, he should be informed that he is not expected to act simply as an observer; and also that the purposes of his presence are, first, to advise the person being interviewed and to observe whether or not the interview is being conducted properly and fairly, and, secondly, to facilitate communication with the person being interviewed. (See paragraph 11.16)

10. If the detention of a mentally disordered or mentally handicapped person is reviewed by a review officer or a superintendent, the appropriate adult must, if available at the time be given opportunity to make representations to the officer about the need for continuing detention. (See paragraphs 15.1 and 15.2)

11. If the custody officer charges a mentally disordered or mentally handicapped person with an offence or takes such other action as is appropriate when there is sufficient evidence for a prosecution this must be done in the presence of the appropriate adult. The written notice embodying any charge must be given to the appropriate adult. (See paragraphs 16.1 to 16.3)

12. An intimate search of a mentally disordered or mentally handicapped person may take place only in the presence of the appropriate adult of the same sex, unless the person specifically requests the presence of a particular adult of the opposite sex. (See Annex A, paragraph 4)

Notes for guidance

E1 In the case of persons who are mentally disordered or mentally handicapped, it may in certain circumstances be more satisfactory for all concerned if the appropriate adult is someone who has experience or training in their care rather than a relative lacking such qualifications. But if the person himself prefers a relative to a better qualified stranger his wishes should if practicable be respected. (See Note 1E)

E2 *The purpose of the provision at paragraph 3.13 is to protect the rights of a mentally disordered or mentally handicapped person who does not understand the significance of what is being said to him. It is not intended that, if such a person wishes to exercise the right to legal advice, no action should be taken until the appropriate adult arrives. (See Note 3G)*

E3 *It is important to bear in mind that although persons who are mentally disordered or mentally handicapped are often capable of providing reliable evidence, they may, without knowing or wishing to do so, be particularly prone in certain circumstances to provide information which is unreliable, misleading or self-incriminating. Special care should therefore always be exercised in questioning such a person, and the appropriate adult involved, if there is any doubt about a person's mental state or capacity. Because of the risk of unreliable evidence, it is important to obtain corroboration of any facts admitted whenever possible. [See Note 11B]*

E4 *Because of the risks referred to in Note E3, which the presence of the appropriate adult is intended to minimise, officers of superintendent rank or above should exercise their discretion to authorise the commencement of an interview in the adult's absence only in exceptional cases, where it is necessary to avert an immediate risk of serious harm. [See Annex C, sub-paragraph 1(b) and Note C1]*

Appendix XII

National Health Service and Community Care Act 1990

Section 47

47.—(1) Subject to subsections (5) and (6) below, where it appears to a local authority that any person for whom they may provide or arrange for the provision of community care services may be in need of any such services, the authority—

(a) shall carry out an assessment of his needs for those services; and

(b) having regard to the results of that assessment, shall then decide whether his needs call for the provision by them of any such services.

(2) If at any time during the assessment of the needs of any person under subsection (1)(a) above it appears to a local authority that he is a disabled person, the authority—

(a) shall proceed to make such a decision as to the services he requires as is mentioned in section 4 of the Disabled Persons (Services, Consultation and Representation) Act 1986 without his requesting them to do so under that section; and

(b) shall inform him that they will be doing so and of his rights under that Act.

(3) If at any time during the assessment of the needs of any person under subsection (1)(a) above, it appears to a local authority—

(a) that there may be a need for the provision to that person by such District Health Authority as may be determined in accordance with regulations of any services under the National Health Service Act 1977, or

National Health Service and Community Care Act 1990 c. **19**

(b) that there may be a need for the provision to him of any services which fall within the functions of a local housing authority (within the meaning of the Housing Act 1985) which is not the local authority carrying out the assessment,

the local authority shall notify that District Health Authority or local housing authority and invite them to assist, to such extent as is reasonable in the circumstances, in the making of the assessment; and, in making their decision as to the provision of the services needed for the person in question, the local authority shall take into account any services which are likely to be made available for him by that District Health Authority or local housing authority.

(4) The Secretary of State may give directions as to the manner in which an assessment under this section is to be carried out or the form it is to take but, subject to any such directions and to subsection (7) below, it shall be carried out in such manner and take such form as the local authority consider appropriate.

(5) Nothing in this section shall prevent a local authority from temporarily providing or arranging for the provision of community care services for any person without carrying out a prior assessment of his needs in accordance with the preceding provisions of this section if, in the opinion of the authority, the condition of that person is such that he requires those services as a matter of urgency.

(6) If, by virtue of subsection (5) above, community care services have been provided temporarily for any person as a matter of urgency, then, as soon as practicable thereafter, an assessment of his needs shall be made in accordance with the preceding provisions of this section.

(7) This section is without prejudice to section 3 of the Disabled Persons (Services, Consultation and Representation) Act 1986.

(8) In this section—

"disabled person" has the same meaning as in that Act; and

"local authority" and "community care services" have the same meanings as in section 46 above.

Appendix XIII

Criminal Procedure (Insanity and Unfitness to Plead) Act 1991

1.—(1) A jury shall not return a special verdict under section 2 of the Trial of Lunatics Act 1883 (acquittal on ground of insanity) except on the written or oral evidence of two or more registered medical practitioners at least one of whom is duly approved.

(2) Subsections (2) and (3) of section 54 of the Mental Health Act 1983 ("the 1983 Act") shall have effect with respect to proof of the accused's mental condition for the purposes of the said section 2 as they have effect with respect to proof of an offender's mental condition for the purposes of section 37(2)(a) of that Act.

2. For section 4 of the Criminal Procedure (Insanity) Act 1964 ("the 1964 Act") there shall be substituted the following sections—

> **4.**—(1) This section applies where on the trial of a person the question arises (at the instance of the defence or otherwise) whether the accused is under a disability, that is to say, under any disability such that apart from this Act it would constitute a bar to his being tried.
>
> (2) If, having regard to the nature of the supposed disability, the court are of opinion that it is expedient to do so and in the interests of the accused, they may postpone consideration of the question of fitness to be tried until any time up to the opening of the case for the defence.
>
> (3) If, before the question of fitness to be tried falls to be determined, the jury return a verdict of acquittal on the count or each of the counts on which the accused is being tried, that question shall not be determined.
>
> (4) Subject to subsections (2) and (3) above, the question of fitness to be tried shall be determined as soon as it arises.
>
> (5) The question of fitness to be tried shall be determined by a jury and—
>
> (a) where it falls to be determined on the arraignment of the accused and the trial proceeds, the accused shall be tried by a jury other than that which determined that question;
>
> (b) where it falls to be determined at any later time, it shall be determined by a separate jury or by the jury by whom the accused is being tried, as the court may direct.

(6) A jury shall not make a determination under subsection (5) above except on the written or oral evidence of two or more registered medical practitioners at least one of whom is duly approved.

4A.—(1) This section applies where in accordance with section 4(5) above it is determined by a jury that the accused is under a disability.

(2) The trial shall not proceed or further proceed but it shall be determined by a jury—

(a) on the evidence (if any) already given in the trial; and

(b) on such evidence as may be adduced or further adduced by the prosecution, or adduced by a person appointed by the court under this section to put the case for the defence,

whether they are satisfied, as respects the count or each of the counts on which the accused was to be or was being tried, that he did the act or made the omission charged against him as the offence.

(3) If as respects that count or any of those counts the jury are satisfied as mentioned in subsection (2) above, they shall make a finding that the accused did the act or made the omission charged against him.

(4) If as respects that count or any of those counts the jury are not so satisfied, they shall return a verdict of acquittal as if on the count in question the trial had proceeded to a conclusion.

(5) A determination under subsection (2) above shall be made—

(a) where the question of disability was determined on the arraignment of the accused, by a jury other than that which determined that question; and

(b) where that question was determined at any later time, by the jury by whom the accused was being tried.

3. For section 5 of the 1964 Act there shall be substituted the following section—

5.—(1) This section applies where—

(a) a special verdict is returned that the accused is not guilt by reason of insanity; or

(b) findings are recorded that the accused is under a disability and that he did the act or made the omission charged against him.

(2) Subject to subsection (3) below, the court shall either—

(a) make an order that the accused be admitted, in accordance with the provisions of Schedule 1 to the Criminal Procedure (Insanity and Unfitness to Plead) Act 1991, to such hospital as may be specified by the Secretary of State; or

(b) where they have the power to do so by virtue of section 5 of that Act, make in respect of the accused such one of the following orders as they think most suitable in all the circumstances of the case, namely—

(i) a guardianship order within the meaning of the Mental Health Act 1983;

(ii) a supervision and treatment order within the meaning of Schedule 2 to the said Act of 1991; and

(iii) an order for his absolute discharge.

(3) Paragraph (b) of subsection (2) above shall not apply where the offence to which the special verdict or findings relate is an offence the sentence for which is fixed by law.

4.—(1) For section 6 of the Criminal Appeal Act 1968 ("the 1968 Act") there shall be substituted the following section—

6.—(1) This section applies where, on an appeal against conviction, the Court of Appeal, on the written or oral evidence of two or more registered medical practitioners at least one of whom is duly approved, are of opinion—

(a) that the proper verdict would have been one of not guilty by reason of insanity; or
(b) that the case is not one where there should have been a verdict of acquittal, but there should have been findings that the accused was under a disability and that he did the act or made the omission charged against him.

(2) Subject to subsection (3) below; the Court of Appeal shall either—

(a) make an order that the appellant be admitted, in accordance with the provisions of Schedule 1 to the Criminal Procedure (Insanity and Unfitness to Plead) Act 1991, to such hospital as may be specified by the Secretary of State; or
(b) where they have the power to do so by virtue of section 5 of that Act, make in respect of the appellant such one of the following orders as they think most suitable in all the circumstances of the case, namely—

(i) a guardianship order within the meaning of the Mental Health Act 1983;
(ii) a supervision and treatment order within the meaning of Schedule 2 to the said Act of 1991; and
(iii) an order for his absolute discharge.

(3) Paragraph (b) of subsection (2) above shall not apply where the offence to which the appeal relates is an offence the sentence for which is fixed by law.

(2) For section 14 of the 1968 Act there shall be substituted the following sections—

14.—(1) This section applies where, on an appeal under section 12 of this Act, the Court of Appeal, on the written or oral evidence of two or more registered medical practitioners at least one of whom is duly approved, are of opinion that—

(a) the case is not one where there should have been a verdict of acquittal; but
(b) there should have been findings that the accused was under a disability and that he did the act or made the omission charged against him.

(2) Subject to subsection (3) below, the Court of Appeal shall either—

(a) make an order that the appellant be admitted, in accordance with the provisions of Schedule 1 to the Criminal Procedure (Insanity and Unfitness to Plead) Act 1991, to such hospital as may be specified by the Secretary of State; or

(b) where they have the power to do so by virtue of section 5 of that Act, make in respect of the appellant such one of the following orders as they think most suitable in all the circumstances of the case, namely—

(i) a guardianship order within the meaning of the Mental Health Act 1983;

(ii) a supervision and treatment order within the meaning of Schedule 2 to the said Act of 1991; and

(iii) an order for his absolute discharge.

(3) Paragraph (b) of subsection (2) above shall not apply where the offence to which the appeal relates is an offence the sentence for which is fixed by law.

14A.—(1) This section applies where, in accordance with section 13(4)(b) of this Act, the Court of Appeal substitute a verdict of acquittal and the Court, on the written or oral evidence of two or more registered medical practitioners at least one of whom is duly approved, are of opinion—

(a) that the appellant is suffering from mental disorder of a nature or degree which warrants his detention in a hospital for assessment (or for assessment followed by medical treatment) for at least a limited period; and

(b) that he ought to be so detained in the interests of his own health or safety or with a view to the protection of other persons.

(2) The Court of Appeal shall make an order that the appellant be admitted for assessment, in accordance with the provisions of Schedule 1 to the Criminal Procedure (Insanity and Unfitness to Plead) Act 1991, to such hospital as may be specified by the Secretary of State.

Criminal Procedure (Insanity and Unfitness to Plead) Act 1991 (a)

3–1420 5. Orders under 1964 and 1968 Acts.—(1) The provisions of Schedule 1 (**b**) to this Act shall apply in relation to the following orders, namely—

(*a*) any order made by the Crown Court under section 5 of the 1964 Act that the accused be admitted to hospital; and

(*b*) any order made by the Court of Appeal under section 6, 14 or 14A of the 1968 Act that the appellant be so admitted.

(2) The 1983 Act shall have effect, in its application to guardianship orders within the meaning of that Act, as if the reference in section 37(1) to a person being convicted before the Crown Court of such an offence as is there mentioned included references—

(*a*) to a special verdict being returned that the accused is not guilty by reason of insanity, or to findings being recorded that the accused is under a disability and that he did the act or made the omission charged against him; and

(*b*) to the Court of Appeal being, on an appeal against conviction or under section 12 of the 1968 Act, of such opinion as is mentioned in section 6(1) or 14(1) of that Act;

and in relation to guardianship orders made by virtue of this subsection, references in the 1983 Act to the offender shall be construed accordingly.

(3) The power to make a supervision and treatment order within the meaning given by Part I of Schedule 2(c) to this Act shall be exercisable, subject to and in accordance with Part II of that Schedule—

(*a*) by the Crown Court in cases to which section 5 of the 1964 Act applies; and

(*b*) by the Court of Appeal in cases to which section 6 or 14 of the 1968 Act applies;

and Part III of that Schedule shall have effect with respect to the revocation and amendment of such orders.

(4) Section 1A(1) of the Powers of Criminal Courts Act 1973 shall have effect, in its application to orders for absolute discharge, as if—

(*a*) the reference to a person being convicted by or before a court of such an offence as is there mentioned included such references as are mentioned in subsection (2)(*a*) and (*b*) above; and

(*b*) the reference to the court being of the opinion that it is inexpedient to inflict punishment included a reference to it thinking that an order for absolute discharge would be most suitable in all the circumstances of the case.

SCHEDULE 2

Section 5(3)

SUPERVISION AND TREATMENT ORDERS

PART I

PRELIMINARY

1.—(1) In this Schedule "supervision and treatment order" means an order requiring the person in respect of whom it is made ("the supervised person")—

(*a*) to be under the supervision of a social worker or probation officer ("the supervising officer") for a period specified in the order of not more than two years; and

(*b*) to submit, during the whole of that period or such part of it as may be specified in the order, to treatment by or under the direction of a registered medical practitioner with a view to the improvement of his mental condition.

(2) The Secretary of State may by order direct that sub-paragraph (1) above shall be amended by substituting, for the period specified in that sub-paragraph as originally enacted or as previously amended under this sub-paragraph, such period as may be specified in the order.

(3) An order under sub-paragraph (2) above may make in paragraph 8(2) below any amendment which the Secretary of State thinks necessary in consequence of any substitution made by the order.

(4) The power of the Secretary of State to make orders under sub-paragraph (2) above shall be exercisable by statutory instrument which shall be subject to annulment in pursuance of a resolution of either House of Parliament.

Part II

Making and Effect of Orders

Circumstances in which orders may be made

2.—(1) The court shall not make a supervision and treatment order unless it is satisfied—

(*a*) that, having regard to all the circumstances of the case, the making of such an order is the most suitable means of dealing with the accused or appellant; and

(*b*) on the written or oral evidence of two or more registered medical practitioners, at least one of whom is duly approved, that the mental condition of the accused or appellant—

(i) is such as requires and may be susceptible to treatment; but

(ii) is not such as to warrant the making of an admission order within the meaning of Schedule 1 to this Act, or the making of a guardianship order within the meaning of the 1983 Act.

(2) The court shall not make a supervision and treatment order unless it is also satisfied—

(*a*) that the supervising officer intended to be specified in the order is willing to undertake the supervision; and

(*b*) that arrangements have been made for the treatment intended to be specified in the order (including arrangements for the reception of the accused or appellant where he is to be required to submit to treatment as a resident patient).

(3) Subsections (2) and (3) of section 54 of the 1983 Act shall have effect with respect to proof of a person's mental condition for the purposes of sub-paragraph (1) above as they have effect with respect to proof of an offender's mental condition for the purposes of section 37(2)(*a*) of that Act.

Making of orders and general requirements

3.—(1) A supervision and treatment order shall either—

(*a*) specify the local social services authority area in which the supervised person resides or will reside, and require him to be under the supervision of a social worker of the local social services authority for that area; or

(*b*) specify the petty sessions area in which that person resides or will reside, and require him to be under the supervision of a probation officer appointed for or assigned to that area.

(2) Before making such an order, the court shall explain to the supervised person in ordinary language—

(*a*) the effect of the order (including any requirements proposed to be included in the order in accordance with paragraph 5 below); and

(*b*) that a magistrates' court has power under paragraphs 6 to 8 below to review the order on the application either of the supervised person or of the supervising officer.

(3) After making such an order, the court shall forthwith give copies of the order to a probation officer assigned to the court, and he shall give a copy—

(*a*) to the supervised person;

(*b*) to the supervising officer; and

(*c*) to the person in charge of any institution in which the supervised person is required by the order to reside.

(4) After making such an order, the court shall also send to the clerk to the justices for the petty sessions area in which the supervised person resides or will reside ("the petty sessions area concerned")—

(*a*) a copy of the order; and

(*b*) such documents and information relating to the case as it considers likely to be of assistance to a court acting for that area in the exercise of its functions in relation to the order.

(5) Where such an order is made, the supervised person shall keep in touch with the supervising officer in accordance with such instructions as he may from time to time be given by that officer and shall notify him of any change of address.

Obligatory requirements as to medical treatment

4.—(1) A supervision and treatment order shall include a requirement that the supervised person shall submit, during the whole of the period specified in the order or during such part of that period as may be so specified, to treatment by or under the direction of a registered medical practitioner with a view to the improvement of his mental condition.

(2) The treatment required by any such order shall be such one of the following kinds of treatment as may be specified in the order, that is to say—

(*a*) treatment as a resident patient in a hospital or mental nursing home, not being a special hospital within the meaning of the National Health Service Act 1977;

(*b*) treatment as a non-resident patient at such institution or place as may be specified in the order; and

(*c*) treatment by or under the direction of such registered medical practitioner as may be so specified;

but the nature of the treatment shall not be specified in the order except as mentioned in paragraph (*a*), (*b*) or (*c*) above.

(3) While the supervised person is under treatment as a resident patient in pursuance of a requirement of a supervision and treatment order, the supervising officer shall carry out the supervision to such extent only as may be necessary for the purpose of the revocation or amendment of the order.

(4) Where the medical practitioner by whom or under whose direction the supervised person is being treated for his mental condition in pursuance of a supervision and treatment order is of the opinion that part of the treatment can be better or more conveniently given in or at an institution or place which—

(*a*) is not specified in the order; and

(*b*) is one in or at which the treatment of the supervised person will be given by or under the direction of a registered medical practitioner,

he may, with the consent of the supervised person, make arrangements for him to be treated accordingly.

(5) Such arrangements as are mentioned in sub-paragraph (4) above may provide for the supervised person to receive part of his treatment as a resident patient in an institution or place notwithstanding that the institution or place is not one which could have been specified for that purpose in the supervision and treatment order.

(6) Where any such arrangements as are mentioned in sub-paragraph (4) above are made for the treatment of a supervised person—

(*a*) the medical practitioner by whom the arrangements are made shall give notice in writing to the supervising officer, specifying the institution or place in or at which the treatment is to be carried out; and

(*b*) the treatment provided for by the arrangements shall be deemed to be treatment to which he is required to submit in pursuance of the supervision and treatment order.

Optional requirements as to residence

5.—(1) Subject to sub-paragraphs (2) and (3) below, a supervision and treatment order may include requirements as to the residence of the supervised person.

(2) Before making such an order containing any such requirement, the court shall consider the home surroundings of the supervised person.

(3) Where such an order requires the supervised person to reside in an approved hostel or any other institution, the period for which he is so required to reside shall be specified in the order.

PART III

REVOCATION AND AMENDMENT OF ORDERS

Revocation of order in interests of health or welfare

6. Where a supervision and treatment order is in force in respect of any person and, on the application of the supervised person or the supervising officer, it appears to a magistrates' court acting for the petty sessions area concerned that, having regard to circumstances which have arisen since the order was made, it would be in the interests of the health or welfare of the supervised person that the order should be revoked, the court may revoke the order.

Amendment of order by reason of change of residence

7.—(1) This paragraph applies where, at any time while a supervision and treatment order is in force in respect of any person, a magistrates' court acting for the petty sessions area concerned is satisfied that the supervised person proposes to change, or has changed, his residence from the area specified in the order to another local social services authority area or petty session area.

(2) Subject to sub-paragraph (3) below, the court may, and on the application of the supervising officer shall, amend the supervision and treatment order by substituting the other area for the area specified in the order.

(3) The court shall not amend under this paragraph a supervision and treatment order which contains requirements which in the opinion of the court, cannot be complied with unless the supervised person continues to reside in the area specified in the order unless, in accordance with paragraph 8 below, it either—

(*a*) cancels those requirements; or

(*b*) substitutes for those requirements other requirements which can be complied with if the supervised person ceases to reside in that area.

Amendment of requirements of order

8.—(1) Without prejudice to the provisions of paragraph 7 above, but subject to sub-paragraph (2) below, a magistrates' court for the petty sessions area concerned may, on the application of the supervised person or the supervising officer, by order amend a supervision and treatment order—

(*a*) by cancelling any of the requirements of the order; or

(*b*) by inserting in the order (either in addition to or in substitution for any such requirement) any requirement which the court could include if it were the court by which the order was made and were then making it.

(2) The power of a magistrates' court under sub-paragraph (1) above shall not include power to amend an order by extending the period specified in it beyond the end of two years from the date of the original order.

Amendment of requirements in pursuance of medical report

9.—(1) Where the medical practitioner by whom or under whose direction the supervised person is being treated for his mental condition in pursuance of any requirement of a supervision and treatment order—

(*a*) is of the opinion mentioned in sub-paragraph (2) below; or

(*b*) is for any reason unwilling to continue to treat or direct the treatment of the supervised person,

he shall make a report in writing to that effect to the supervising officer and that officer shall apply under paragraph 8 above to a magistrates' court for the petty sessions area concerned for the variation or cancellation of the requirement.

(2) The opinion referred to in sub-paragraph (1) above is—

(*a*) that the treatment of the supervised person should be continued beyond the period specified in the supervision and treatment order;

(*b*) that the supervised person needs different treatment, being treatment of a kind to which he could be required to submit in pursuance of such an order;

(*c*) that the supervised person is not susceptible to treatment; or

(*d*) that the supervised person does not require further treatment.

Supplemental

10.—(1) On the making under paragraph 6 above of an order revoking a supervision and treatment order, the clerk to the court shall forthwith give copies of the revoking order to the supervising officer.

(2) A supervising officer to whom in accordance with sub-paragraph (1) above copies of a revoking order are given shall give a copy to the supervised person and to the person in charge of any institution in which the supervised person was required by the order to reside.

11.—(1) On the making under paragraph 7 or 8 above of an order amending a supervision and treatment order, the clerk to the court shall forthwith—

(*a*) if the order amends the supervision and treatment order otherwise than by substituting a new area or a new place for the one specified in the supervision and treatment order, give copies of the amending order to the supervising officer;

(*b*) if the order amends the supervision and treatment order in the manner excepted by paragraph (*a*) above, send to the clerk to the justices for the new petty sessions area concerned—
  (i) copies of the amending order; and
  (ii) such documents and information relating to the case as he considers likely to be of assistance to a court acting for that area in exercising its functions in relation to the order;

and in a case falling within paragraph (*b*) above, the clerk to the justices for that area shall give copies of the amending order to the supervising officer.

(2) Where in accordance with sub-paragraph (1) above copies of an order are given to the supervising officer, he shall give a copy to the supervised person and to the person in charge of any institution in which the supervised person is or was required by the order to reside.

Appendix XIV

Magistrates Court Act 1980

30 Remand for medical examination

(1) If, on the trial by a magistrates' court of an offence punishable on summary conviction with imprisonment, the court is satisfied that the accused did the act or made the omission charged but is of opinion that an inquiry ought to be made into his physical or mental condition before the method of dealing with him is determined, the court shall adjourn the case to enable a medical examination and report to be made and shall remand him; but the adjournment shall not be for more than 3 weeks at a time where the court remands him in custody nor for more than 4 weeks at a time where it remands him on bail.

(2) Where on an adjournment under subsection (1) above the accused is remanded on bail, the court shall impose conditions under paragraph (*d*) of section 3(6) of the Bail Act 1976 and the requirements imposed as conditions under that paragraph shall be or shall include requirements that the accused—

(*a*) undergo medical examination by a duly qualified medical practitioner or, where the inquiry is into his mental condition and the court so directs, two such practitioners; and

(*b*) for that purpose attend such an institution or place, or on such practitioner, as the court directs and, where the inquiry is into his mental condition, comply with any other directions which may be given to him for that purpose by any person specified by the court or by a person of any class so specified.

(3) The Costs in Criminal Cases Act 1973 shall apply to a duly qualified medical practitioner who makes a report otherwise than in writing for the purposes of this section as it applies to a person called to give evidence, and shall so apply notwithstanding that the proceedings for the purposes of which the report is made are not proceedings to which section 1 of that Act applies.

Appendix XV

Prosecution of Offences Act 1985 s. 23

23 Discontinuance of proceedings in magistrates' courts

(1) Where the Director of Public Prosecutions has the conduct of proceedings for an offence, this section applies in relation to the preliminary stages of those proceedings.

(2) In this section, "preliminary stage" in relation to proceedings for an offence does not include—

(*a*) in the case of a summary offence, any stage of the proceedings after the court has begun to hear evidence for the prosecution at the trial;

(*b*) in the case of an indictable offence, any stage of the proceedings after—

(i) the accused has been committed for trial; or

(ii) the court has begun to hear evidence for the prosecution at a summary trial of the offence.

(3) Where, at any time during the preliminary stages of the proceedings, the Director gives notice under this section to the clerk of the court that he does not want the proceedings to continue, they shall be discontinued with effect from the giving of that notice but may be reviewed by notice given by the accused under subsection (7) below.

(4) Where, in the case of a person charged with an offence after being taken into custody without a warrant, the Director gives him notice, at a time when no magistrates' court has been informed of the charge, that the proceedings against him are discontinued, they shall be discontinued with effect from the giving of that notice.

(5) The Director shall, in any notice given under subsection (3) above, give reasons for not wanting the proceedings to continue.

(6) On giving any notice under subsection (3) above the Director shall inform the accused of the notice and of the accused's right to require the proceedings to be continued; but the Director shall not be obliged to give the accused any indication of his reasons for not wanting the proceedings to continue.

(7) Where the Director has given notice under subsection (3) above, the accused shall, if he wants the proceedings to continue, give notice to that effect to the clerk of the court within the prescribed period; and where notice is so given the proceedings shall continue as if no notice had been given by the Director under subsection (3) above.

(8) Where the clerk of the court has been so notified by the accused he shall inform the Director.

(9) The discontinuance of any proceedings by virtue of this section shall not prevent the institution of fresh proceedings in respect of the same offence.

(10) In this section "prescribed" means prescribed by rules made under section 144 of the Magistrates' Courts Act 1980.

Appendix XVI

Crown Prosecution Service

Mentally Disordered Offenders

1 CODE FOR CROWN PROSECUTORS, 8 (v)

(a) The Crown Prosecution Service endorses the spirit and objectives of the Home Office Circular on Provision for Mentally Disordered Offenders (Home Office Circular No. 66/1990). Accordingly, where there is evidence to establish that an accused or a person under investigation was suffering from mental disorder at the time the offence was committed, the Crown Prosecutor will observe the principle that prosecution will not be appropriate in the circumstances unless it is overridden by the wider public interest, including in particular the gravity of the offence. Other material considerations will include the circumstances of any previous offences, and such relevant information concerning the nature of the person's condition, the likelihood of his further offending, and the availability of suitable alternatives to prosecution as may be provided.

(b) Where criminal proceedings are contemplated or have been instituted and the Crown Prosecutor is provided with a medical report to the effect that the strain of criminal proceedings may lead to a considerable worsening of the accused's mental health, such report should receive anxious consideration. This is a difficult field because in some instances the accused may have become mentally disturbed or depressed by the mere fact that his misconduct has been discovered and the Crown Prosecutor may be dubious about a prognosis that criminal proceedings will adversely affect his condition to a significant extent. Where, however, the Crown Prosecutor is satisfied that the probable effect on the defendant's mental health outweighs the considerations in favour of a prosecution in that particular case, he should not hesitate to advise against or discontinue proceedings. An independent medical report may be sought, but should generally be reserved for cases of such gravity as plainly to require prosecution unless the examination provides clear evidence that such a course would be likely to result in a permanent worsening of the accused's condition. The accused's mental state will, of course, be relevant in considering any issue of mens rea or fitness to plead.

2 HOC No. 66/90 PROVISION FOR MENTALLY DISORDERED OFFENDERS

(1) CPS will participate in any inter-agency arrangement set up to advise and agree procedures to meet the recommendations of the Circular.

(2) CPS will seek to agree a policy on diversion with chief officers of police locally.

(3) The routine disclosure of CPS files (paragraphs 7 and 11 of Annex C to the Circular) will not take place.

(4) CPS will not take part in inter-agency case conferences or discussions about how to proceed in individual cases except where asked for advice by the police, in the usual way.

(5) Police files should include any information (in writing or summary) supplied by an agency advising of a defendant's condition and prognosis, or advocating a particular approach or disposal — with reasons.

(6) The police should include in the CPS file a brief summary of the reasons for instituting proceedings (or recommending a course of action when seeking pre-charge advice).

(7) The police should ensure that the prosecutor knows what arrangements have been put in hand to have the defendant assessed for any purpose; or any other matters about which the prosecutor needs to know, for his own or the Court's information.

(8) Police bail (with or without 'conditions' of residence or treatment) should be kept short, for early review of the case. The CPS file should show clearly any informal conditions agreed.

(9) Bail Information Schemes are the preferred vehicle for advice to prosecutors as to factors in favour of bail.

(10) Otherwise, such advice should be in writing, from an authoritative source and be accurate and reliable.

(11) Inappropriate use of cautioning should be avoided, when N.F.A. would be the proper alternative to prosecution.

Note: these guidelines are under review.

Appendix XVII

Bail Act 1976 s. 4

Bail for accused persons and others

4 General right to bail of accused persons and others

(1) A person to whom this section applies shall be granted bail except as provided in Schedule 1 to this Act.

(2) This section applies to a person who is accused of an offence when—
(*a*) he appears or is brought before a magistrates' court or the Crown Court in the course of or in connection with proceedings for the offence, or
(*b*) he applies to a court for bail in connection with the proceedings.
This subsection does not apply as respects proceedings on or after a person's conviction of the offence or proceedings against a fugitive offender for the offence.

(3) This section also applies to a person who, having been convicted of an offence, appears or is brought before a magistrates' court to be dealt with under section 6 or section 16 of the Powers of Criminal Courts Act 1973 (breach of requirement of probation or community service order).

(4) This section also applies to a person who has been convicted of an offence and whose case is adjourned by the court for the purpose of enabling inquiries or a report to be made to assist the court in dealing with him for the offence.

(5) Schedule 1 to this Act also has effect as respects conditions of bail for a person to whom this section applies.

(6) In Schedule 1 to this Act "the defendant" means a person to whom this section applies and any reference to a defendant whose case is adjourned for inquiries or a report is a reference to a person to whom this section applies by virtue of subsection (4) above.

(7) This section is subject to [section 41 of the Magistrates' Courts Act 1980] (restriction of bail by magistrates court in cases of treason).

SCHEDULES

SCHEDULE 1

Section 4

Persons Entitled to Bail: Supplementary Provisions

Part 1

Defendants Accused or Convicted of Imprisonable Offences

Defendants to whom Part 1 applies

1. Where the offence or one of the offences of which the defendant is accused or convicted in the proceedings is punishable with imprisonment the following provisions of this Part of this Schedule apply.

Exceptions to right to bail

2. The defendant need not be granted bail if the court is satisfied that there are substantial grounds for believing that the defendant, if released on bail (whether subject to conditions or not) would—
(*a*) fail to surrender to custody, or
(*b*) commit an offence while on bail, or
(*c*) interfere with witnesses or otherwise obstruct the course of justice, whether in relation to himself or any other person.

3. The defendant need not be granted bail if the court is satisfied that the defendant should be kept in custody for his own protection or, if he is a child or young person, for his own welfare.

4. The defendant need not be granted bail if he is in custody in pursuance of the sentence of a court or of any authority acting under any of the Services Acts.

5. The defendant need not be granted bail where the court is satisfied that it has not been practicable to obtain sufficient information for the purpose of taking the decisions required by this Part of this Schedule for want of time since the institution of the proceedings against him.

6. The defendant need not be granted bail if, having been released on bail in or in connection with the proceedings for the offence, he has been arrested in pursuance of section 7 of this Act.

Exception applicable only to defendant whose case is adjourned for inquiries or a report

7. Where his case is adjourned for inquiries or a report, the defendant need not be granted bail if it appears to the court that it would be impracticable to complete the inquiries or make the report without keeping the defendant in custody.

Restriction of conditions of bail

8.—(1) Subject to sub-paragraph (3) below, where the defendant is granted bail, no conditions shall be imposed under subsections (4) to (7) of section 3 of this Act unless it appears to the court that it is necessary to do so for the purpose of preventing the occurrence of any of the events mentioned in paragraph 2 of this Part of this Schedule or, in the case of a condition under subsection (6)(*d*) of that section, that it is necessary to impose it to enable inquiries or a report to be made into the defendant's physical or mental condition [or, where the condition is that the defendant reside in a bail hostel or probation hostel, that it is necessary to impose it to assess his suitability for being dealt with for the offence in a way which would involve a period of residence in a probation hostel].

(2) Sub-paragraph (1) above also applies on any application to the court to vary the conditions of bail or to impose conditions in respect of bail which has been granted unconditionally.

(3) The restriction imposed by sub-paragraph (1) above shall not [apply to the conditions required to be imposed under section 3(6A) of this Act or] operate to override the direction in [section 30(2) of the Magistrates' Courts Act 1980] to a magistrates' court to impose conditions of bail under section 3(6)(*d*) of this Act of the description specified in [the said section 30(2)] in the circumstances so specified.

Decisions under paragraph 2

9. In taking the decisions required by paragraph 2 of this Part of this Schedule, the court shall have regard to such of the following considerations as appear to it to be relevant, that is to say—

(*a*) the nature and seriousness of the offence or default (and the probable method of dealing with the defendant for it),
(*b*) the character, antecedents, associations and community ties of the defendant,
(*c*) the defendant's record as respects the fulfilment of his obligations under previous grants of bail in criminal proceedings,
(*d*) except in the case of a defendant whose case is adjourned for inquiries or a report, the strength of the evidence of his having committed the offence or having defaulted,

as well as to any others which appear to be relevant.

[9A.—(1) If—

(*a*) the defendant is charged with an offence to which this paragraph applies; and
(*b*) representations are made as to any of the matters mentioned in paragraph 2 of this Part of this Schedule; and
(*c*) the court decides to grant him bail,

the court shall state the reasons for its decision and shall cause those reasons to be included in the record of the proceedings.

(2) The offences to which this paragraph applies are—

(*a*) murder;
(*b*) manslaughter;
(*c*) rape;
(*d*) attempted murder; and
(*e*) attempted rape.]

9B. Where the court is considering exercising the power conferred by section 128A of the Magistrates' Courts Act 1980 (power to remand in custody for more than 8 clear days), it shall have regard to the total length of time which the accused would spend in custody if it were to exercise the power.]

Part II

Defendants Accused or Convicted of Non-Imprisonable Offences

Defendants to whom Part II applies

1. Where the offence or every offence of which the defendant is accused or convicted in the proceedings is one which is not punishable with imprisonment the following provisions of this Part of this Schedule apply.

Exceptions to right to bail

2. The defendant need not be granted bail if—

(*a*) it appears to the court that, having been previously granted bail in criminal proceedings, he has failed to surrender to custody in accordance with his obligations under the grant of bail; and

(*b*) the court believes, in view of that failure, that the defendant, if released on bail (whether subject to conditions or not) would fail to surrender to custody.

3. The defendant need not be granted bail if the court is satisfied that the defendant should be kept in custody for his own protection or, if he is a child or young person, for his own welfare.

4. The defendant need not be granted bail if he is in custody in pursuance of the sentence of a court or of any authority acting under any of the Services Act.

5. The defendant need not be granted bail if, having been released on bail in or in connection with the proceedings for the offence, he has been arrested in pursuance of section 7 of this Act.

Glossary

APPROPRIATE ADULT

If a Custody Officer has any reason to believe that a person in custody is suffering from a mental disorder, or mental handicap or cannot understand the significance of questions put to him, the Custody Officer must inform an Appropriate Adult of the detention and ask the Appropriate Adult to come to the police station. The Appropriate Adult should be present when the person is interviewed.

An Appropriate Adult may be a relative, guardian, or some person responsible for the care of a mentally disordered offender, someone who has experience of dealing with mentally disordered or handicapped people; in the last resort it may be any person over eighteen not employed by the Police. (See PACE Code of Practice, Code C, Annexe E p. 134)

APPROVED SOCIAL WORKER

An Approved Social Worker is a qualified social worker who has undertaken additional training on mental health to a recognised national standard.

Approved Social Worker status is reviewed by the employing social services department, every five years, following assessment of ability and performance.

An Approved Social Worker is authorised to apply for compulsory admission to hospital of a person who is detainable under the MHA 1983, under one of the civil sections of the Act.

BAIL INFORMATION OFFICER

A Bail Information Officer is usually a Probation Officer whose task is to verify for the Court, information about any person applying for bail under the terms of the Bail Act 1976. This verified information about, for example, a person's job or home address, will inform the decision of the Crown Prosecution Service about whether or not to oppose the granting of bail, and the decision of the Magistrates to grant or refuse bail.

CARE PROGRAMME APPROACH

A care programme should be provided for every person who has come into contact with the mental health services. The care programme should name a key worker who is primarily responsible for ensuring that the care package detailed in the care programme is delivered.

The care programme should be drawn up in consultation with the recipient of the service. If a person is discharged from the care of the mental health services, effective arrangements should be in place to ensure that person receives the continuing care and support required before the discharge is made. This does not always happen.

COMMUNITY PSYCHIATRIC NURSE (CPN)

A Community Psychiatric Nurse is a practitioner who provides psychiatric nursing and assessment in health centres, GP surgeries, out-patients clinics, and people's own homes.

CRIMINAL RESPONSIBILITY

The law assumes that everyone is responsible for their actions unless it can be proved otherwise. The burden of proof for this defence lies with the offender but it need only be on the 'balance of probabilities' as opposed to beyond all reasonable doubt.

If at the time of the offence it can be shown that the mentally disordered offender, because of his mental illness or learning disability, did not know what he was doing or understand that what he was doing was wrong, it can be argued that he is not criminally responsible for his actions.

CUSTODY OFFICER

Custody Officers are police officers — usually of acting or substantive rank of sergeant who are responsible for decisions relating to the treatment of persons in police custody in designated police stations.

The duties of custody officers are set out in PACE 1983, S36, 37, 38 and 39 and in the PACE Code of Practice, Code C. Annexe E refers particularly to people with mental disorders and mental handicap.

The Custody Officer maintains a custody record, decides whether the detention of a suspect is warranted and whether there is sufficient evidence to charge the suspect.

If the detention of a suspect is extended beyond 24 hours, the detention must be authorised by a superintendent. Beyond 36 hours, approval must be obtained from a Magistrates Court.

DESIGNATED/HOLDING POLICE STATIONS

Police stations are divided into two categories by S35 and 36 PACE 1986.

Designated, and non-designated. Non-designated police stations may hold prisoners for up to six hours. After that time if the detained person is not released, he or she will be transferred to a designated police station.

DOCTORS APPROVED UNDER S12 OF MHA 1983

A S12 Approved Doctor is a medical practitioner approved by the Secretary of State, under the provisions of S12 (2) MHA 1983 as having special experience in the diagnosis or treatment of mental disorder.

Recommendations for admission to hospital under Part II of the MHA 1983, relating to compulsory admissions, must be made by two doctors, of whom one must be a S12 Approved Doctor.

There are no specific qualifications required for S12 Approval, applicants are not always qualified in psychiatry.

Applications are made initially to a local advisory panel of consultants who then make recommendations to the regional health authority who maintain the register of Approved Doctors.

Approval remains in place for five years after which re-approval must be sought.

FORENSIC MEDICAL EXAMINER

Formerly known as a Police Surgeon, the FME is usually a GP, but may also be a S12 Approved Doctor. The FME will be called to the police station to examine and assess persons in custody at the request of the custody officer.

The FME will determine such issues as whether the person in custody is fit to be detailed, and to be interviewed.

MANIC DEPRESSION

Definition

Manic depression is characterised by dramatic mood swings. Periods of deep depression may alternate with periods of over-active or excited behaviour, known as mania. These episodes may alternate with periods of relative stability of varying length.

Symptoms

Symptoms include extreme changes of mood, when 'high' people will be talkative, energetic and euphoric. They may be very extravagant and spend large sums of money. They may have difficulty sleeping and become irritable and angry. They will not appreciate that their behaviour has changed.

Causes

These include a bio-chemical imbalance in the brain which pre-disposes a person to breakdown following a stressful event which acts as a trigger. Some psychiatrists believe manic depression is caused by severe emotional damage in childhood or excessive reaction to the problems of life.

Treatment

Lithium Carbonate may be prescribed as a preventative measure. Frequent blood tests are required to monitor toxicity. Major tranquillizers may be used when the mania is most extreme.

Psychotherapy is not considered helpful by Psychiatrists.

MENTAL IMPAIRMENT/LEARNING DISABILITY/MENTAL HANDICAP

Definition

Mental Health Act 1983 defines mental impairment and severe mental impairment as a state of arrested or incomplete development of mind, which includes significant or severe impairment of intelligence and social functioning and is associated with abnormally aggressive or seriously irresponsible conduct on the part of the person concerned.

Symptoms
The symptoms of mental handicap vary enormously from those with a mild learning disability who may not be able to read or write well, to those with a very low level of intellectual functioning.

Causes
Mental handicap is usually caused by damage to or incomplete develoment of the brain, occurring before or during birth. Mental handicap can be caused by brain damage resulting from infection, head injury, deprivation of oxygen, or vaccination damage. Mental handicap should be distinguished from mental illness. However, there may be an ovelap as people who are mentally impaired may also suffer from mental illness.

Treatment
Mental handicap is not curable. Drugs may be prescribed to control symptoms such as fits. Behavioural therapy, special education and social support may improve social functioning and reduce anti-social behaviour.

PSYCHOPATHIC DISORDER

Definition
Psychopathic disorder is one of the four categories of mental disorder listed in S1(2) of the Mental Health Act 1983 and defined as a 'persistent disorder or disability of mind (whether or not including significant impairment of intelligence) which results in abnormally aggressive or seriously irresponsible conduct on the part of the person concerned'. There is no widely accepted definition of psychopathy. It is a term which is rarely used in psychiatry outside the criminal justice system.

Symptoms
Symptoms vary enormously and may include antisocial behaviour, lack of conscience, no feelings of remorse and an inability to control the desire for immediate gratificiation of desires. Psychopathy is also associated with an inability to form relationships.

Causes
Possibly a genetic predisposition, compounded by neurological damage at birth and environmental factors such as abuse and poverty.

Treatment
Many psychopathic disorders are considered 'untreatable' and the person cannot be compulsorily treated under the Mental Health Act 1983. Treatments which have been tried include drugs, ECT, psychosurgery, psychotherapy, behaviour modification, either singly or in combination with other treatments.

For further information see: Dolan and Coid,1993, *Psychopathic and Antisocial Personality Disorders*, London: Gaskells.

REGIONAL SECURE UNIT

Regional Secure Units are secure mental hospitals. They were established following the Butler Report in 1976. By 1996 there will be about 1000 places nationally in Regional Secure Units.

The RSUs offer assessment and intensive therapy and rehabilitation for mentally disordered offenders with treatable mental illness. The maximum length of stay is two years. The average length of stay is eight months.

The service may be funded on a per case or block contract basis by district health authority purchasing trusts.

There may be a long waiting list for admission.

SCHIZOPHRENIA

Definition

Schizophrenia is the name psychiatrists use to describe a range of symptoms. These include thought disorder, auditory hallucinations and delusions.

Symptoms

The first symptoms usually appear between the ages of fifteen and twenty years. The symptoms may last for a few weeks or may continue to affect a person for the rest of his/her life.

Causes

There are conflicting theories about the causes of schizophrenia. These include a chemical malfunction of the brain, a genetic disposition and a range of socio-economic causes including poverty and unemployment.

Treatment

The treatment usually prescribed is major tranquillizers. This treatment may have distressing side effects including nausea, a dry mouth, lethargy and permanent damage to the central nervous system resulting in Parkinsons disease-like symptoms.

SPECIAL HOSPITAL

There are three special hospitals in England, providing a service to England and Wales. Ashworth, Broadmoor and Rampton.

They currently have a patient population of about 1500 which is declining. They provide a service to people with mental illness and learning disability, usually as long-term patients.

SUPERVISION REGISTERS

Supervision registers were established in each mental health Trust area in 1994. The aim of the registers is to ensure patients with care programmes, who pose a risk to themselves or others, receive adequate care, support and supervision in the community. Patients will be registered if they present a significant risk of suicide, serious violence or severe self-neglect.

Patients should be informed orally and in writing of their inclusion on the supervision register. Continued inclusion in the register should be considered at every review of the care programme, at least every six months. The patient or an advocate can request removal of his/her name from the register but the decision to withdraw a patient from the register is the responsibility of the relevant consultant psychiatrist.

References

Bingham, M. (1992) Provision for Mentally Disordered Offenders — a Scheme for Humberside MSc dissertation (unpublished).

Bynoe, I. (1992) *Treatment Care and Security*, report, MIND Publications.

Cheston, L. (1993) 'A safety net full of holes'. *Probation Journal*, Dec. p. 203.

Collins, Jean (1993) 'Free from care', *Community Care* 11 Nov. p. 18.

Grounds, A. (1990) *Prison Service Journal*, Nov.

Gordon, R. (1993) *Community Care Assessments*, Longman.

Gunn, J., Madden, T. and Swinton, M. (1991) 'Treatment needs of prisoners with psychiatric disordes'. *British Medical Journal*, **303**, Aug.

Hedderman, C. (1993) Panel Assessment Schemes for Mentally Disordered Offenders (Home Office Research and Planning Unit Paper 176, Home Office research and statistics research bulletin No. 34), HMSO.

Home Office (1976) Bail Act, HMSO.

Home Office (1983) Mental Health Act, HMSO.

Home Office (1984) Police and Criminal Evidence Act, HMSO.

Home Office (1990) National Health Service and Community Care Act, HMSO.

Home Office Circular 66/1990 Provision for Mentally Disordered Offenders, HMSO.

Home Office (1991) Insanity and Unfitness to Plead Act, HMSO.

Home Office (1991) Criminal Justice Act, HMSO.

Joseph, P. (1992) Report of the Establishment of a Psychiatric Assessment Scheme at Great Marlborough Street and Bow Street Magistrates Court, Home Office.

Miles, X. (1993) *R* v *Glamorgan County Council* in Cheston, L. 'A safety net full of holes'. *Probation Journal*, Dec. p. 203.

The Reed Report (1992) CM 2088. Review of Health and Social Services for Mentally Dissordered Offenders and Others Requiring Similar Services, HMSO.

Villeneuve, Louise (1993) *Housing with Care and Support*, MIND Publications.

Bibliography

Bynoe, I. (1992) *Treatment, Care and Security*, London: MIND Publications.

Cavadino, P. and Gibson, B. (1991) *Criminal Justice Act 1991*, Winchester: Waterside.

Cavadino, P. and Gibson, B. (1994) *Bail: the Law, Best Practice and Debate*, Winchester: Waterside.

Dolan, B. and Coid, J. (1993) *Psychopathic and Anti-social Personality Disorders*, London: Gaskell.

Gordon, R. (1993) *Community Care Assessments: a Practical Legal Framework*, London: Longman.

Gunn, J., Madden, T. and Swinton, M. (1991) *Mentally Disordered Prisoners*, London: Home Office.

Hedderman, C. (1993) 'Panel Assessment Schemes', London: Home Office — Home Office Research and Planning Unit Paper 76.

Herbst, K. and Gunn, J. (1991) *The Mentally Abnormal Offender*, London: Butterworth-Heineman.

Hoggett, R. (1990) *Mental Health Law*, London: Sweet and Maxwell.

Jones, H. (1992) Report off the British Telethon Enquiry into the Relationship between Mental Health, Homelessness and the Criminal Justice System, London: NACRO.

Jones, R. (1991) *Mental Health Act Manual* (third edition), London: Sweet and Maxwell.

NACRO (1993) *Diverting Mentally Disturbed Offenders from Prosecution*.

The Reed Report (1992) Review of Health and Social Services for Mentally Disordered Offenders and Others Requiring Similar Services, HMSO, CM2088.

Zander, M. (1990) *Police and Criminal Evidence Act*, London: Sweet and Maxwell.

Index